The Beckoning of the West

A
Lancashire
Odyssey

by Norman Cunliffe

Published
in co-operation with the
North Lancashire District Methodist History Group

Contents

ISBN 0-9520233-0-X

Preface

Some eight years ago, following the sudden death of Rev. Gordon Sutcliffe, it fell to me to organise an event at Poulton le Fylde on behalf of the North Lancashire Methodist History Group about local Methodist history. At that time I had only been a member of the group for less than a year and most of what I knew about Methodist history was centred on Blackpool and had been acquired through my interest in local history in general as a member of the Blackpool and Fylde Historical Society.

In order to prepare myself for the event I therefore began to examine the impact of Methodism over a wider area so as to include Poulton, Thornton and the western part of the Fylde, but the more research I did the more I came to realise that what occurred in these places had been influenced by events further afield in earlier years. It was thus that I gradually came to recognise how Methodism began to first find its way into Lancashire and then spread westwards some 250 years ago. I hope that the results of what I have discovered will provide a link between the beginnings of Methodism nationally and the early history of the chapels and societies within the county that are known to the reader and thereby help create a better understanding of our heritage.

I would like to express my sincere thanks to those whose names are shown below for the kind assistance given to me in various ways; by providing valuable information and sharing their knowledge and expertise; by loaning me books or allowing me to have access to deeds, documents and other papers; and by giving me their advice and encouragement. I am also greatly indebted to Eric Wolstenholme of the North Lancashire Methodist History Group for the line drawings and cover design, which he so willingly offerred to do when asked. Finally, especial thanks are due to my wife Beryl, who has patiently borne the hours I have spent in either study, Library or Record Office.

Thanks to:-
the staff of the Reference Departments of the Blackpool Central Library, the Blackburn Library, the Keighley Library and the Todmorden Library; the staff of the Lancashire Library Services; the staff of the Methodist Archive and Research Centre; and the staff of the Lancashire Record Office, who I have particularly overworked; the Committee and members of the North Lancashire Methodist History Group: Ken Bowden, Kevin Butterworth, Rev. John Carr, Colin Dews, Tony Difford, Rev. Eric W. Dykes, Henry Kirby, Rev. Brian Kirkpatrick, Ted Lightbown, Geoffrey E. Milburn, Michael Priestley, Alan Rose, Harry Sandford, Doug Seed, Helen Spencer, Christine Storey and Dr. Angus Winchester.

Norman Cunliffe, 1992

River Ribble

A 59

M6

A 677

● MELLOR

B 6230

● SHORROCKS
GREEN

BLACKBURN ◉

A 675

River Darwen

TOP O'
TH' COAL
● PITS

HOGHTON●
TOWER

LOWER
DARWEN

FENISCOWLES ●

BRINDLE
●

BRIMMICROFT●

● MOULDING
WATER

A 6061

A 674

OVER ●
DARWEN

MARSH ●
LANE

● ●LAUND

OLLERTON

0   1   2

SCALE — MILES

EW

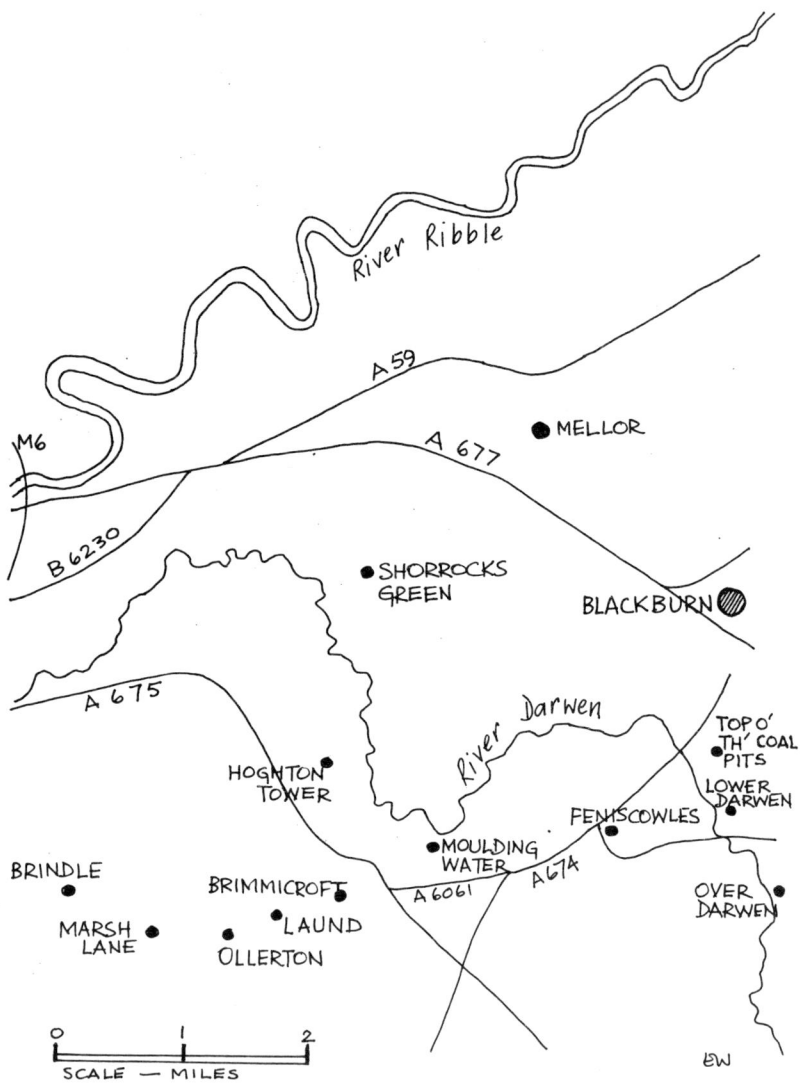

The area South and West of Blackburn showing places
of Methodist influence in the 18th Century.

4

Chapter One

Early Ventures

Methodism took a long time to reach Blackpool. It took forty years for it to travel the four miles from Poulton. It only found a home in Poulton in 1792, a year after the death of John Wesley at the age of 87 and fifty three years since the creation of the first Methodist Society.

The journey of Methodism to the western part of Lancashire took a considerable length of time as it slowly progressed from the Pennine hills in the eastern part of the county, but before it could even begin the journey it had first to reach the North of England.

Although the Methodists had been meeting in Religious Societies for a number of years the first that could be regarded as being exclusively Methodist was formed in 1739 at the New Room, Bristol, from an amalgamation of two groups which had been meeting in houses, after earlier being influenced by the outdoor preaching of George Whitefield and Wesley. Soon after opening, this Society increased its membership to around five hundred and was subsequently divided into Classes under a leader for ease of collecting monies for the repayment of the debt and for maintaining pastoral care. The introduction of these membership classes and leaders became the pattern for all future Societies and has remained an integral part of Methodism to this day.

Following the success of the Bristol Society and the formation of another in London the following year Wesley began to seek ways of expanding the Methodist movement. He realised that there were insufficient 'methodist' clergymen to develop the work so, after overcoming earlier doubts, he began to choose laymen as travelling preachers to spread the message to other parts of the country. They were appointed to preaching Circuits and were encouraged to set up Methodist Societies if there was a request to do so. In addition Wesley himself began to itinerate until he was covering between four and five thousand miles a year on horseback. It was from such circumstances that Methodism became established in the North of England and eventually Lancashire.

It must be emphasised that, despite the unorthodox approach, as a clergyman Wesley did not believe that his mission of evangelism was in any way inconsistent with the doctrines and practices of the Church of England. He professed himself, as did his brother Charles, a loyal member of the Church throughout his life. His endeavours were directed to revitalizing the Church from within and he made a point of encouraging all his followers to attend the services at the Parish Church, especially the service of Holy Communion. Whenever he preached outdoors he did so at a time other than when the parish service was appointed to be held. Whenever he could and when invited he would preach in the Parish Church, but unfortunately as the years progressed he was invited less and less, although there were some of the clergy who valued his work and gave him their support. Most of the clergy did not care for the outdoor preaching of the Methodists, which proclaimed a love for all men, whatever their status. They objected to the crowds that heard them and the religious fervour and lusty hymn singing which occurred uninvited in their parishes. Some were belligerent, but within the boundaries of modern day Lancashire he did find support.

Wesley visited Lancashire on many occasions and is known to have preached in Preston four times between 1780 and his death. He had, however, visited the Preston area or passed near to it on other occasions in the years previous, when journeying in the North of England. His Journal records that he was in Lancaster in May 1759 after being in North Wales a week earlier, [1] and it also shows that on some of his journeys he stayed with a friend from these parts, James Edmondson. [2] For a time James lived at Chipping, but then moved to Brookhouse, Bilsborrow, where Wesley is known to have spent the night. It was probably through Edmondson that he was introduced to the incumbent of Chipping, Rev. John Milner, from whose pulpit he preached in 1752. [3]

On an earlier visit Milner met him at Bolton and from there rode to Ribchester, where by appointment they met with a number of clergymen. Wesley records that he spent"....one or two hours in serious and useful conversation", before going on to stay the night at Chipping vicarage. [4] On another occasion when Wesley was visiting his friend he was prevented from preaching at the morning service by several persons who barred his way to the pulpit and reading desk, so a shortened service was conducted by Milner, after which he and Wesley proceeded to the vicarage followed by a good part of the congregation. There Wesley was able to address the crowd and similarly in the evening. [5] Milner was at one with his fellow cleric in promoting the message of the Gospel and wished others could be of the same mind, but unfortunately most of the local clergy were not so inclined. Whenever possible he would accompany Wesley on his journeys about North Lancashire and on more than one occasion he attended the Conference of Methodists when it was held at Leeds.

Besides being the incumbent at Chipping, Milner held the post of the King's Preacher, an office created in Queen Elizabeth's day. Such preachers, then twelve in number, were an authorised itinerancy within the Church of England and were appointed "......to spread true religion through the Kingdom", with the position commanding a separate salary. [6] These aims seem to have been consistent with those that Wesley was trying to achieve. Milner had been a King's Preacher for Lancashire since 1748, otherwise he was a devoted parish priest at Chipping from 1739 until his death in 1777 at the age of sixty seven. His memorial tablet can be found in the Parish Church.

Despite Wesley's many journeys into Lancashire however, the main thrust of

Methodism in the county came from the West Riding of Yorkshire and from Derbyshire. In these and other neighbouring areas the Evangelical Movement took an early hold, where in addition to the Dissenting sects, the Inghamites and the Moravians were especially influential. This was before the Methodism as preached by John Wesley had reached these parts. Therefore, in order to appreciate and understand the progress of Methodism as it spread through Lancashire, it is first necessary to look at the wider evangelistic movement, together with the evangelists who were preaching in the neighbouring counties.

The precursor of this new wave of evangelism in Yorkshire was one of the 'Holy Club' members and associate of John Wesley in America, the Rev. Benjamin Ingham. Two months after he had returned from that country he experienced a special call to evangelism and the following month he wrote to say that he had no other thought but of returning to minister to the Indians again. But soon his mind was changed when he became aware that there was a great need amongst the folk of his native Yorkshire, where he had been preaching since his return. By the end of 1737 he had held meetings in about thirty places. (7)

Benjamin was born at Ossett in June 1712, son of William Ingham, and after attending Batley Grammar School he went to Queen's College, Oxford, from where he obtained his B.A. Degree in 1734. A year later he was ordained by Bishop Potter at Christ Church, four months before setting out for America. Earlier in February 1734, whilst he was still unordained, he had found time to help some of the children in his home town to learn to read and he became involved in a school which was founded there the following year. (8) Ossett was also the place where he began to preach on his return from America, both in the church and in private homes.

Like Wesley, he had taken a great deal of interest in the Moravians and with a view to learning more about them and their faith, he joined Wesley on the visit to various Moravian centres in Germany during the summer of 1738. Almost five months were to pass before Ingham returned to London, where he then spent most of the last two months of the year in contact with the growing Evangelical Societies, including the one at Fetter Lane with its increasing Moravian influence. Early in the following year he was back evangelizing in Yorkshire with a good deal of success preaching to crowded congregations, many of which were composed of people from the working classes. At first he was invited to preach in the churches near his home town and his message began to persuade his hearers to change their way of life. He visited the people in their homes and then began to form a number of classes in the vicinity. Gradually however, whilst his popularity with the populace increased, the co-operation which he had received from the clergy diminished, until finally in June 1739, as a result of a meeting at Wakefield Parish Church, he was barred from preaching in any of the churches within the Diocese of York. (9) Thus he was prompted into preaching wherever he could, both

7

indoors and out, farm buildings and houses, and gradually his societies increased in number.

Whilst he had been in Germany a friendship had developed with John Toltschig, one of the Moravian leaders, and before he left Ingham asked if it would be possible for his friend to accompany him to England and stay with him for a while. The proposed visit did not materialise, for Toltschig could not be spared, and the request did not get fulfilled until late the following year, when the Moravian paid a brief visit to Yorkshire, where he helped Ingham with his work and became popular with the ordinary folk. Prior to this, he did have a visit from another Moravian, Peter Bohler, who assisted for a while. Somehow Ingham, who greatly admired the work of his Moravian friends, was still able to maintain a friendly relationship with Wesley, despite the latter feeling cooler towards the Brethren, but there were others from the 'methodist' group who gave them much more of their support, including James Hutton, John Cennick and William Delamotte. The latter also helped Ingham over a period of eight months from November 1739 with the work in Yorkshire. (10)

Sometime the following year Ingham "..discovered something new in his heart.......he had never before experienced". (11) In writing of this event to Hutton, who lived in London, he asked if his friend Toltschig could once again help him for "..many souls in Yorkshire have of late found grace" and there were many others who were anxious to see him for a second time. (12) Again the time was not opportune, but Ingham did find other lay preachers to help him - first David Taylor and then John Nelson.

John Nelson became a preacher prior to Christmas 1740 in and about his home town of Birstal on his return from London, where he had been working as a stonemason. (13) He and his family had resided in the capital for some years, but eventually his wife and children returned home permanently, whilst John spent a further period there after a brief stay in Yorkshire. It was during this latter period in London that he went to hear George Whitefield preach at Moorfields in the Spring of 1739, and from then on he took an interest in the Methodists, listening to John Wesley whenever he had the opportunity. A few months later he had a conversion experience and before long was able to speak with Wesley for the first time about his new found faith when they met in St. Paul's Cathedral.

Over a year was to pass following this meeting before he felt the need to return to his native Yorkshire, where he immediately began the work of telling his friends and relations about his experiences, and also preached to them. His message must have been appealing for soon his brother had been converted, then six neighbours, to be followed shortly after by his wife. Within three weeks there were seventeen of them. These results encouraged him to take up regular preaching from his home, mainly in the evenings after he had finished his work, and by so doing became the first of those who followed Wesley to take up regular lay preaching in Yorkshire. Tradition records that he often preached with his hammer and trowel hanging from a string tied round his leather apron. As more and more people went to hear him so more of them responded to his message, until there were on average six or seven per week having their lives renewed.

Some time after he got home, during the early part of the next year, he went to hear David Taylor, who was preaching at one of Ingham's Societies nearby, and after listening to him Nelson remarked about the dryness of the message, which prompted Taylor to ask for his reasons. Nelson simply told him to go and listen to the preaching of John Wesley and then he would understand.

David Taylor, who was employed for a time as a coachman and footman by members of the Earl of Huntingdon's family, had been converted through the preaching of Ingham about 1738/39, which so pleased Lady Huntingdon that she encouraged him to take up preaching himself. Soon he was to be found travelling about on such a mission in the vicinity of his home at Woodhouse Eaves, near Loughborough, and later over a wider area in Leicestershire and the neighbouring counties. Shortly after speaking with Nelson he appears to have taken note of his comments, for soon he was to be found preaching Wesley's doctrine in Sheffield and Derbyshire, where many were awakened and converted. Wesley was travelling with him in June 1741 about the county borders of Derbyshire, Nottinghamshire and Leicestershire. (14) In November he was preaching in the High Peak District at the invitation of one of his converts John Bennet, who lived at Chinley. He preached first at Chapel en le Frith, where some of the locals disturbed him by ringing the bells, then he visited Chinley End and Marple, Cheshire. Returning to Chapel en lc Frith a week later he preached to a large multitude on the common and in recording the event Dr. James Clegg, minister of the Independent Chapel in that place, stated "I think it does not become us to give these Methodists any disturbance or opposition". Of Taylor he wrote of him as being"..a pious, zealous and well meaning man of great assurance, but little learning or knowledge". (15) Unfortunately however, his preaching was once again gradually influenced by Ingham and the Moravians, as was Nelson's for a time. Throughout his preaching life Taylor tended to be a waverer.

The Inghamites and the Moravians together were without doubt the dominant evangelists in the area, for as yet Wesley himself had not been to these parts, and did not do so until May 1742. John Nelson was still evangelizing on his own when the Moravian, Peter Bohler, came again to Yorkshire and was so impressed with the work he was doing that he told him he would speak to Ingham to see if John could be taken on as one of his assistants. This was soon accomplished and Nelson was given permission to preach in all of Ingham's Societies. The offer was taken up and for a while they worked together but the 'marriage' did not last long, because of differences which arose between the two men over policy and doctrine. Nelson, following the lead given by John Wesley, advised those to whom he preached and who were still members of the Church of England to continue attending church and receive the sacraments, whilst Ingham, being more under the influence of the Moravians, advised to the contrary. This caused confusion in the minds of the hearers and resulted in many absencing themselves from the Established Church on the Sabbath. In addition, towards the end of 1741, at one of the meetings which Ingham held every month at Gomersal for the representatives from his Societies, the decision was made that all the young preachers were to withdraw from preaching for a month pending a further review. It was thought that by having too much preaching they were in danger of fostering persecution. Nelson, however, felt that so long as the 'devil' was still active he had a duty to preach and he continued to do so, which prompted Ingham to deny him access to his preaching places. As a result, by the end of January 1742, Nelson had separated from Ingham and the Moravian influence, and from then on he was a Wesley man.

The rest of that year he travelled further afield and carried his message to Armley, Leeds, Wakefield, Halifax and many other places in the West Riding, encouraging Methodist Societies to start up wherever he could. This was especially true after the visit of Wesley, who he had not seen since leaving London, and who stayed overnight at Birstal on his way to and from Newcastle on Tyne. This was the first of what were to be almost annual visits that Wesley made to those parts. He thought a great deal of John Nelson and the work that he was doing about his home. He described Birstal as a town with a new face "because of the testimony of a plain man".

About the time of Nelson's separation from Ingham, David Taylor was once again preaching to crowds in North Derbyshire and Cheshire, where he was allowed into the pulpit of Mr. Smith of Stockport. Dr. Clegg also wrote about this tour and the error of Taylor's preaching, and he prayed for those of his own congregation who flocked to hear the evangelist and became influenced by the doctrine they heard or were otherwise disturbed by his utterances. (16) Later in the Spring both Taylor and Ingham were touring the area again, and this time John Bennet, much to the displeasure of his parents, accompanied them as they went about preaching. They visited Woodley and Dukinfield in Cheshire, followed by Ashton under Lyne in Lancashire before going to Manchester. (17)

John Bennet, who was to figure prominently in this first decade of Methodism, was born about 1714 and was reasonably well educated. (18) When he was 17 or thereabouts he began to study for the Christian ministry in the Presbyterian Church, but he gave it up to become a clerk to one of the local Justices of the Peace, where he remained for a few years before starting in business as a carrier between Macclesfield and Sheffield, with occasional trips further afield. At the end of 1741, whilst on a visit to Sheffield Races, he went along to hear Taylor preach, with the intention of ridiculing him. Instead

10

he was struck by Taylor's enthusiasm and as a result became the instrument of the latters visit to Derbyshire at that time. Bennet's education, together with the administrative and accountancy skills he acquired running a business, were to prove an asset in the work that lay ahead.

For the following six months he continued about home with his business and attended meetings and preaching services in the area until, in the early part of the following year, he paid a visit to Birstal in order to see Nelson. Together they discussed their beliefs, but soon found that they did not agree on all matters, with Bennet leaning to the teachings of the Moravians, which was to be expected because of his associations with Ingham and Taylor. However, after being advised by Nelson to read certain scriptures, he spent time in thought and contemplation until he eventually became of the same mind as the stonemason. Resulting from this meeting, Bennet very soon invited the lay preacher to spend a few days touring and preaching in Lancashire, Cheshire and Derbyshire. By arrangement they met at Marsden, high on the Pennines, and then went to Hopkin Pit, where Nelson preached. Then from Lancashire he went on to preach at Woodley, Cheshire, before finding out that arrangements had been made for him to preach at Manchester Cross the following Sunday. This he did in the afternoon to a crowd estimated to be about two thousand, but unfortunately some were unsympathetic and created a disturbance, which resulted in stones being thrown, one of which hit Nelson on the head, injuring him. Disturbing though it may have been, this Spring day in 1743 was a momentous occasion for it was when the first Lancashire town of any size had the Methodism of Wesley proclaimed in it. The same period was also momentous for John Bennet because on 18 March, as recorded in his Diary, he gave a word of exhortation for the first time in public. A month later he took an even greater step and went to meet John Wesley, who was on his way back from Newcastle and, not too far from Chesterfield, it was decided that he would become an Assistant Preacher for Wesley.

Meanwhile the Moravian Brethren at their Synod of 1741 had decided that their future sphere of influence was to be concentrated in Yorkshire, rather than London, "..in the footsteps of the Methodist and on the field where Mr. Ingham had hitherto been active". (19) The use of 'Methodist' in this statement is somewhat ambiguous, for it is not clear whether reference was being made to the work of John Nelson, or whether it related solely to Ingham and his associates Taylor and W.Delamotte, who evangelized in the 'Methodist' manner and were thought of by many as Methodists. Ingham had already begun to widen his sphere of influence, but he was anxious to travel even further afield. He felt that in order to do so the groups which he had founded in Yorkshire needed caring for, so consequently a combined meeting of all his followers was convened and he asked them if they would agree to the Moravians working directly amongst them, to which they readily agreed. An official request was sent to the Moravian leaders which resulted in them making the decision to form a band of workers known as the 'Yorkshire Congregation', which was to take over Ingham's Societies. These Moravian workers, comprising twenty six men and women, left London in July 1742 under the leadership of Brother Spangenburg, and on arriving in Yorkshire set about formalising the agreement, which up to then had only been done verbally. Subsequently a document was prepared and signed by twelve hundred Yorkshire followers of Benjamin Ingham, formally handing over his Societies to the Moravian Church, which by now had taken over a farm building at Smith House, Lightcliffe, near Halifax, as its headquarters.

In the 'History of the Moravian Church' the Ingham Societies which participated in the agreement were shown to be mostly concentrated in an area of approximately fifteen miles square to the west and south of Leeds. They were listed as Pudsey, Great Horton, Holbeck, Lightcliffe, Wyke, Halifax, Mirfield, Hightown, Dewsbury, Wakefield, Leeds, Wortley, Farnley, Cleckheaton, Great Gomersal and Baildon - sixteen in all, which is considerably less than the fifty or so places, within the same area, which a year or two earlier were recorded as being either Societies or preaching places of the evangelist.

When the takeover by the Moravian Brethren had been accomplished, Ingham was then able to consider extending his evangelistic work. Just prior to giving up his 'old' Societies he had been encouraged to go to the Settle district by his friend William Delamotte, who when he was helping Ingham in 1740 had visited this area and done some preaching. This was probably at the request of Lawrence Batty of Laneshaw, an associate, who had accompanied Ingham, Delamotte and others when they were evangelizing in Cambridge and Bedford at the end of 1738 and the next year. Lawrence's brothers, William and Christopher, had been helped by the visit of Delamotte and it was because of them that Ingham was encouraged to visit the area. It was whilst he was returning from a second visit there at the beginning of 1743 that he was met by a Joseph Gawkroger of Wycoller, who invited him to visit Lancashire and preach to some of the folk who had heard about him. Within a few days he was heading in that direction. His journey there took him by way of Haworth, where he stayed the night and also preached at the request of the evangelical curate, Rev. William Grimshaw. The following day he visited Wycoller and Colne, where he also preached. During the next three years Ingham made occasional visits into Lancashire, but from Spring 1746 he began work there in earnest until he had founded Societies in around twenty places. (20)

The Rev. William Grimshaw had only been serving as perpetual curate of Haworth for less than a year when he met Ingham, but within that time his church had undergone a complete transformation. Grimshaw, who had earlier experienced a spiritual renewal, succeeded two unpopular clergymen, and was able to lead a revival almost immediately on arriving there and the church often became crowded to the doors and beyond. On some occasions he would have to preach in the churchyard to accommodate all his hearers. In the summer following Ingham's visit he regularly went out preaching within his parish to groups of people who assembled together in local cottages. This development was somewhat akin to the Class Meetings of the Methodist Societies, but they appear to have been set up as a natural response to the need created by his evangelism, and enabled him to have a better pastoral oversight than would have been possible through the larger church gatherings. On the other hand the possibility that these cottage meetings were set up as a result of conversations with Ingham should not be overlooked. William had not yet had any direct contact with the Methodists who followed Wesley, but Ingham would be able to impart something about the organisation to him, and tell him about his own Societies. Grimshaw had deliberately avoided coming into contact with the Methodists and when John Nelson went to preach in the vicinity of Haworth he advised his parishioners not to go to hear him.

Rev. William Grimshaw was a Lancastrian, who had been born at Brindle in 1708, the son of William and Ann. (21) From an early age he attended Blackburn Grammar School, where for much of the time he was taught by Thomas Moon of Kirkham and was also greatly influenced by the headmaster, George Smith of Burnley. When he was in his mid teens he spent a further two years at Heskin Free School, before going on to Christ College, Cambridge, from where he graduated in 1730. After his ordination in the Spring of the following year, he served as curate of Littleborough for a few months before moving to Todmorden, which was then in Lancashire. He remained there for the next ten years, during which time he resolved on more than one occasion to dedicate himself to his calling and he underwent a spiritual experience, which caused him to take up a covenant with God. The fruits of these events were, it seems, harvested in the new ground at Haworth. Notwithstanding, he had an even deeper enrichment in the late summer of 1744 after falling into a semi conscious state, which prompted a further rededication.

It was about this time that he came into contact with another evangelical preacher with a 'Methodist' outlook, who had been preaching in the neighbourhood. He was William Darney and, despite the fact that he was a lay preacher, Grimshaw took the opportunity to speak with him privately about some aspect of faith, and from the meeting a friendship developed. Then, some time later in 1745, Darney preached in Haworth itself, which prompted Grimshaw to record "I have cause to bless God for it". (22) Tradition says that the clergyman helped by reading out a hymn and gave cause for the saying "Mad Grimshaw has turned Scotch Will's clerk". Darney had been converted in Scotland some time before October 1741, for it was then that he received a call to preach but failed to respond. This refusal bothered him, so when he received a similar call the following year he followed it up and by the end of 1743 he had moved into the West Riding of Yorkshire to the vicinity of Pudsey. This Scotsman was a pedlar and clogger by trade and was described as "..a man called Scotch Will, who carry's a pack,

13

sells hankerchers and stockings, often preaches about here......and having some connection with John Nelson". (23) During the first two months of the next year he preached regularly within the town and arranged to "..take down the names of as many as think well to form a Society". (24) During the following month there is every likelihood that Darney came into contact with Charles Wesley, for they were both in Birstal on the same day in the middle of the month. Charles had arrived there on the 11th and the following day spent time "visiting the brethren from house to house". (25) Nationally at this period there was a concern and some amount of antagonism over the support that was being given in certain quarters to the Jacobites, thereby showing a disloyalty to the Crown. Just as Wesley was about to leave Birstal he discovered that he had been named in a summons for speaking in support of the would be King, so he changed his plans and the following day proceeded to Wakefield, where he confronted the Justices of the Peace and cleared his name, before returning to Birstal for the night. Co-incidentally, William Darney was also summoned from Birstal to appear before the Justices at Bradford the next day, because three of his followers as well as seventeen Moravians were to be questioned regarding some supposed form of support they had given to the Pretender. (26)

Although detailed entries in Charles Wesley's Journal regarding the events surrounding his appearance before the Justices and his stay in Birstal make no reference to Darney, considering the similar circumstances in which they were placed and also because of William's association with John Nelson, to whose house Wesley went after his experience, it seems unlikely that they did not see each other. Whether there was contact or not, however, Darney could not yet be considered as one of the Wesley Methodists for he had too much of a leaning towards the Moravians, and it was probably because of this that Nelson had forbidden him to preach in his Societies. The tendency for Darney to try and keep a foot in both camps and his association with Richard Viney led to him going out evangelizing on his own account. He already had two or three Societies of his own, but he began to travel further afield. Before he reached Haworth in 1745, it was recorded that he had been "preaching the Gospel about Bradford, Manningham and other places to the East...". (27) How true the remark was regarding the help given by Grimshaw to Darney, when he was preaching at Haworth, has not been proved, but what is certain is that these two evangelists, ordained and lay, began to work together in and around the Parish of Haworth, in addition to which Grimshaw had the help of two other men, Paul Greenwood from nearby Ponden and Jonathan Maskew. Thus it was that Grimshaw's evangelism in the Haworth area developed spontaneously on similar lines to that of the Methodists.

Chapter Two

The Evangelists Arrive in Lancashire

Darney did not restrict himself to preaching in the Haworth area and soon he had "....pushed the work westwards.... Great numbers in the next parish of Heptonstall were awakened...." Then, at the commencement of 1746 "Lancashire now received its first revival", first Pendle Forest and Colne Parish, then Todmorden and Rossendale, and soon after Haslingden and Rochdale Parish. (1) Gradually groups set up by him in some of these areas came to be known as William Darney's Societies.

Some writers, (2) however, have asserted that Darney had been evangelizing in Lancashire around Todmorden in 1744, although in April and July he is known to have been in the Pudsey and Birstal area. Central to the assertion are the circumstances surrounding the conversion of John Madin, who went to hear Darney when he was preaching at Todmorden. Over the years much has been written about this young man, but the earliest writers seem to have derived their information from a letter, which was written in the form of a memorial following Madin's death and sent to the editor of the Methodist Magazine in November 1809 by Rev. Samuel Taylor of Rochdale and which was published almost two years later. (3) Although the letter contains a couple of anomalies it seems worthwhile to give a precis of part of the memorial as it was written.

John Madin was born near Bacup on 4th December 1724 but "...lived without...God" until he was twenty years old (Therefore on or after 4th December 1744). When he was that age he was persuaded to go to Gauxholme, Todmorden, to hear William Darney, who had arranged to preach in a barn there, and as a result was converted. Darney preached in that neighbourhood (which could infer somewhere other than Gauxholme) for about two weeks and John never missed hearing him, even though it was between five and six miles from his home. (His home was reputed to be at Heap Barn, which was less than four miles from Gauxholme). The visit of Darney was recorded as being in May 1744. (At this date John would still be nineteen). Not only was he converted, but when Darney gathered ten of his hearers together at the end of his visit to form a small Society in the vicinity of Todmorden, John was one of them and he continued attending the meetings there every week for almost one year. Together with others of the Todmorden Society, he was anxious for the gospel to be preached in Rossendale, so later in 1744 at their invitation Darney preached at Heap Barn, but he encountered a good deal of opposition. Despite this setback, Darney was next invited to preach at Miller Barn, near Waterfoot, where it was less antagonistic. He was soon able to form a Society and appointed John Madin as leader.

Gauxholme is shown on Yates's Map of Lancashire about $3/4$ mile south of

Todmorden near to what is now the junction of the Todmorden/Rochdale highway and the road from Bacup to Todmorden. (4) This latter road did not follow the same line in Yates's day, taking a more northerly route from Bacup, via Sharneyford - where Heap Barn was situated - over Flower Scar to Sourhall and Todmorden Edge, from where descent could be made to either Todmorden or Gauxholme. Apart from its mention in the memorial, twelve more years were to elapse before the name of Gauxholme was mentioned in Methodist records concerning its work in the area. The Society that was started "in the vicinity of Todmorden" was not at Gauxholme, but at the home of James and Susan (or Mary) Schofield of Lodge Hall, Calf Lee, which place names appear on the first Ordnance Survey map of the area two miles south of Gauxholme. From other known details and from entries in the Todmorden Parish Registers, 'Everett' has identified the family as James and Susan, but at a much earlier date 'Myles' refers to them as James and Mary. (5) However, a closer look at the Registers shows that there were two families of James and Susan as well as a James and Mary living contemporaneously in the Walsden area. In spite of these variations it appears to be a Schofield home to which Madin made his weekly pilgrimage, and which would be about six miles from Heap Barn.

Identifying John Madin from the Parish records also presents a difficulty, because of the number of Madin families living in Rossendale. None of the baptismal entries for these families relate to any living at Heap Barn or Sharneyford at the time of his birth. Even later, when the earliest records of the Miller Barn Society show the names of its leaders, two John Madins are listed - Senior and Junior. (6) 'Jessop' adds more confusion over the preaching of Darney at Heap Barn, which he informs us was carried out at a farm occupied by Abraham and Elizabeth Earnshaw. (7) If this is correct then the preaching must have been done on the Todmorden side of the nearby boundary. Abraham was married at Todmorden in 1731 to Elizabeth Turner by Rev. William Grimshaw's predecessor, but when he took over he baptized some of their children, who were born over a span of almost twenty years. In the registers the father was shown as a resident of Todmorden Parish. The Earnshaws must have become members of the Methodist Society from a very early date, possibly from the outset of the cause. By 1750 Abraham was certainly a member for his ticket of membership still survives as the earliest extant one in the whole of Methodism. Another ticket issued to his wife a little later also survives. (8) The Earnshaw farm could not have been too far from Todmorden Edge which had become the focal point of the cause in the area and which was visited by Wesley in May 1747. (9) In the membership lists of 1764 the Earnshaws appear in a class whose leader came from nearby Sourhall.

Despite the perplexity surrounding the introduction of Darney's Methodism to Todmorden and Rossendale, what is clear is that, because of his preaching and the zeal and dedication of Madin and others, the 'Methodist' system was able to establish itself there, and later as the work progressed these two men would still have an important part to play.

By the summer of 1746 Grimshaw himself had been to preach beyond his Parish boundary, especially in and around the town of Colne, (10) nine miles to the west of Haworth, near to where classes had already been formed by Darney, and where Benjamin Ingham and his followers were then well established. On one of these visits, Grimshaw is reported to have preached for over two hours to a crowd of people, which brought a complaint from a local publican - no doubt because of a reduction in sales. (11) However, the discontentment on his part was nothing to the disturbances which were to take place in the area over the next two or three years, and which were brought about by the incumbent of Colne, Rev. George White, who stirred up feelings against the evangelical preachers and their followers, all of whom he regarded at Methodists.

Ingham's ministry around here was growing. Besides Colne he had support in Foulridge, Wycoller, Southfield, Barrowford, Clough, Laund, Cowpasture, Wheatley Lane, Widdup and Roughlee. (12) His past experience in setting up and administering Societies in the places where he preached was a distinct advantage to him in this Lancashire venture, but such qualities had not yet been developed by Darney. The Classes and Societies he had created must have been rather more burdensome, for the Scotsman offered them to his fellow evangelist. Ingham, however, declined them and also gave a similar response when asked again in January 1747 whilst on a visit to Haworth, where Darney was also staying. (13)

Five days after Ingham's visit Charles Wesley went to see Grimshaw. This was his second visit, the first occasion having been a few months earlier when both William and his wife were ill with fever. Charles preached from a large house in Haworth on the day of his arrival and lodged the night at Grimshaw's home. Other than expressing his disappointment at not being permitted to preach in the church, Charles's Journal does not state what else was discussed by the two clerics, but in the light of the following days events it seems certain that the work which the Scottish evangelist had been doing was spoken of. Leaving Haworth early the next morning Charles went off to preach in three of Darney's Societies; morning, afternoon and night, before travelling on to Manchester the day after. This was the first step towards these and Darney's other Societies becoming linked with organized Methodism. Although Wesley does not record the names of the places he visited, since he travelled to his final destination via Rochdale, it seems that one of them must have been in the eastern part of Lancashire. (14)

The final step of joining Darney's Societies to Methodism took place just over three months later, when John Wesley and Grimshaw met for the first time, whilst the former was on one of his visits to the north. Prior to their meeting it was obvious that the two men had something in common and this was cemented together over the time that

17

Wesley spent at Haworth, which resulted in the curate throwing in his lot with the Methodists, whilst still continuing as a Parish priest. This is something which Wesley had hoped more of the clergy would have done, for he still cherished the hope that Methodism could be the means by which a renewal of religion would occur within the Established Church. Having a like minded ordained minister in the North of England to oversee the work of the ever growing movement in these parts would certainly have pleased Wesley, but at this time Grimshaw would not be regarded as one of Wesley's Assistants in an administrative sense, but would be more like a father figure, caring for both the travelling preachers in the vicinity and the people to whom they ministered. During his stay Wesley agreed to take over Darney's Societies and then spent three days visiting and preaching at eight of them - Great Harding, Roughlee (where he spent a good deal of time sorting out the waverers and those who had been influenced by Ingham), Hinden, Widdop, Stonsey Gate, Shore, Todmorden Edge and Rossendale(15). Over the next six months Grimshaw was able to visit the old Darney Societies on at least two or three occasions, as well as those about Leeds, Birstal, and, even further afield, the Societies which John Bennet had nurtured at Bolton, Manchester and Cheshire.

Porch entrance to Todmorden Edge South - a Meeting House
of the Quakers and then the Methodists.

18

Chapter Three

Administering the Societies

John Bennet had by now been a Methodist preacher for four years, during which time he had become one of the leaders of the movement in the North of England. 'Everett' in his 'Wesleyan Methodism in Sheffield' states "Few men were more useful in the early stages of Methodism than he". (1) After Wesley had asked him to become one of his preachers, he was soon to be found accompanying Charles Wesley on a tour through Yorkshire and Tyneside, whilst at other times he was travelling in the counties adjacent to his home, preaching and visiting the Societies there. As yet, many of these Societies were lacking a proper identity, receiving visits not only from Bennet, but also from Ingham, Taylor and possibly the Moravians. Sometimes the messages preached by these men were in harmony, but on other occasions the doctrines which they revealed were at variance and caused confusion in the minds of the hearers. This of course applied not only in the area covered by John Bennet, but it occurred in most places which received more than one evangelist. Bennet, however, gathered some of the Societies in Derbyshire, Cheshire and Lancashire together and they soon became known as John Bennet's Societies. (2) By the time he had been preaching for just over a year Wesley thought enough of him to invite him to the Methodist Conference, held in June 1744 at London; one of only four laymen invited. He was also given, with others, additional responsibilities in his role of Assistant Preacher by the 1746 Conference, with authority over the regulation of the Societies, classes and preachers in his Circuit. (3)

The Circuit had now become an essential part of Methodism and allowed for better administration, even though by modern standards the early Circuits were huge. At first it was customary for the travelling preachers to be stationed in a Circuit for two or three months, but eventually the period was extended until it was generally of one year's duration. Some of the stationing of preachers was made at each Conference, which became an annual event, but the plans did not always work out in practice, with even the Wesleys themselves not always travelling to the places at the times planned. Yorkshire was one of the seven original Circuits, but it covered a much wider area than the county and included Derbyshire, Cheshire and Lancashire, amongst others.

At the Conference of 1747 a new classification of preacher was shown under the heading of "those that assist us only in one place", and included in that list was the name of William Darney. (4) The 'in one place' needs to be read in a much wider context than just a town or a village, and more than likely it sometimes would cover part of a Circuit. People whose employment was fixed in one place or area found it difficult to preach too far from their home, except for short tours when they were able to get away from their work. Darney's itinerant occupation allowed him to cover a wider area. In Bennet's Diary, entries reveal that both he and Darney travelled in the Yorkshire Circuit following the 1747 Conference and occasionally accompanied each other or crossed paths as they went from Society to Society. Simply from the references in the Diary, Darney was shown as having been to Chinley, Sheffield, Ewood (Yorks.), Cheshire, Goodshaw, Roughlee, Higham, Heptonstall, nearby Bank, Todmorden Edge, Haworth, Rochdale and Staley Hall between the November and May of the following year. Practically all of these were either former Darney or Bennet Societies.

During this same period Darney also had two notable experiences of a personal nature. The first occurred on the last day of the year when he was apprehended at Heptonstall by the bailiffs and taken to the jail at Halifax. This caused a certain amount of grief amongst the members, but fortunately he escaped any charge and was able to return to Bank that night and speak to those assembled. (5) The second experience was when he married Hannah White at Leeds Parish Church in March 1748. (6) In the few years before he was married Darney did not seem to have any place which he could regard as his permanent home, although he did enjoy long spells of hospitality from his friend Grimshaw at Haworth and also spent some time at Ewood Hall, near Mytholmroyd, which belonged to the Grimshaw family. After his marriage, however, he appears to have had a home between Birstal and Leeds, for Bennet records visiting Hannah Darney there a few months after the marriage, where he gave her a sum of money for her support which had been collected by friends. (7)

Bennet and Darney attended the London Conference of 1748 travelling by way of Newcastle under Lyme, Birmingham, Evesham and Chipping Norton. Amongst the items in the minutes of that Conference were three which had particular reference to the development of Methodism in Lancashire. One was that Darney was acknowledged as a travelling preacher, rather than just 'assisting in one place', and another was that the Circuits had been re-aligned, with the huge Yorkshire Circuit being split and a new one created centred on Cheshire, which also covered Lancashire, Derbyshire, Sheffield and Nottingham. The other item of note expressed a desire to have the Societies more fully and closely united in things spiritual and temporal, but nothing specific was decided upon. (8)

This desire, however, was discussed by the two preachers as they made their way back to the north, and in the mind of Bennet a plan began to develop as to how this might be achieved. The first evidence of his planning is revealed in his Diary for 27th July 1748, which stated that the first Quarterly Meeting in Lancashire was to be held at Todmorden Edge on the 18th October following, and two days later a similar meeting was to be held for Cheshire. The plan was that the leaders of the various classes which formed the Societies within a given area should meet together every three months at a central place so that they could report and deal with the temporal affairs of the group

Todmorden Edge South - Venue of the first Methodist Quarterly Meeting.

on a collective basis. This was a practical way of at least fulfilling part of the desire expressed at the London Conference, but it would also give the preacher, or preachers, an opportunity to nurture more spiritual matters with the leaders. It should be noted that the two meetings arranged were to cover both of the areas where Darney and Bennet had developed their Societies.

On the same day that the Quarterly Meeting notice was made Bennet was preaching at Rochdale when his discourse was interrupted by one of the brethren from Roughlee, who announced that John Jane, a preacher whom Bennet had not yet met, had been taken by force under the instigation of Rev. George White and placed in the stocks before being taken to Mr. Richard Whitehead, a Justice of the Peace, who resided near Blackburn. It was expected that he would be charged as a vagrant and returned to his home county, which was Lincolnshire. Bennet set out early the next day and, after stopping at Hinding to enquire if there was any further news, headed for Blackburn, only to be met after travelling a few miles by the curate of Colne and two of his accomplices, who each carried a pistol. They passed on the news, no doubt with much satisfaction, that the preacher had been sent to the House of Correction at Preston. John Jane had been charged with being "A very disorderly Person wandering about and giving no good account of himself and occasioning Riots and Disturbances in several Parts of this County of Lancaster particularly at Colne on Sunday last occasioning great Tumults and disturbing the Congregation about to attend divine Service". (9)

Hearing this, Bennet proceeded to Preston, where on arrival he was allowed to see the prisoner who he found locked up with the other transgressors. They were able to move about their quarters, but they were handicapped because of the irons into which they had been placed. On being appraised of what the conditions were like Bennet approached a person who he described as "the Keeper of the Prison". This person was in fact the Governor of the House of Correction, a Mr. James Stanley, (10) who lived on the premises with his wife and family, and through him he was able to arrange for Jane to be put in a more agreeable part of the building, after making a payment to cover the costs. These new accommodations were such that Bennet was able to have supper with his fellow preacher and lodge there until the next morning, at which time he set out to try and procure Jane's acquittal or acquire bail. He first travelled to Walton le Dale where he expected that he would be able to obtain one of these concessions from Sir Henry Hoghton, but was surprised that instead of receiving the sympathetic hearing he expected from one who was a supporter of Presbyterianism he received just the opposite, with Sir Henry fuming and raging, likening the Methodists to the Quakers. Having failed at his first attempt he then went to see Richard Whitehead, where eventually late in the day he was able to obtain a letter of release from him by signing a letter of recognizance for £40 to ensure Jane's appearance at the October Quarter Sessions in Preston. (11) After spending a further night with the prisoner, the following morning they were able to set off for Roughlee, but having only one horse between them the going was slow and it was late in the day when they were nearing the town. Here they were met by a friend who gave assistance before finally reaching their destination, where there was great rejoicing and prayerful thanks expressed by the local brethren. The following day the two men set off elsewhere in the Circuit to do that which they had received a call to do - preach.

The Rev. George White was the main agitator and motivator against the Methodists and the Inghamites in the Parish of Colne and vicinity. He did everything in his power to excite the populace into a prejudicial state so that they became physically abusive and he stooped to the point of bribery by plying some of them with drink, whilst hypocritically he blamed the Methodist preachers for disturbing the peace. Furthermore, the example which he set as a Christian minister was deplorable, for he neglected the needs and welfare of the people by absenting himself from the parish for weeks on end. On the Sunday that John Jane had been accused of causing a disturbance the curate preached a sermon against the Methodists at Colne, and he followed this up two weeks later by repeating it at Marsden so as to keep the crowds aroused. As a result the mob was out in force to greet John Wesley, William Grimshaw and other preachers when they came to Roughlee a month later. (12) It was here that they were physically attacked and hit with staves as they attempted to preach to those who wished to hear, and similar treatment was meted out to Ingham and William Batty, who was one of his preachers. After this confrontation had subsided there were other occasions when rioting took place, but gradually the opposition tired of their sport and the trouble faded away. White, besides being an offence to Methodism, also offended in other ways so that within three years after these incidents he had drunk himself into debt, into jail, and into his grave.

At the Quarter Sessions to which Jane was eventually summoned White was his usual arrogant self. Indictments were drawn up by each side, and although the one presented on behalf of Jane was quoshed by the Jury, the Bench were sympathetic toward the preacher and he was discharged. Unfortunately Jane only lived two more years, but his life serving as a Methodist travelling preacher contrasted greatly with that of the Colne curate. (13) Jane accepted his difficult life without question and gave his all in the service to which he had been called. At his death the only possessions which he had were his wearing apparel, the value of which did not even cover his funeral expenses.

The early Methodist preachers did not have an easy life. Most of them were untrained, but they were chosen because of their desire to call people to repentance and to evangelize others into the faith which they had found. Some of those selected were part time itinerants, who preached locally over a smaller area nearer their homes whenever they could, after following their occupation during the day. Wesley kept a tight rein on the preachers and selected or approved of them personally. They were put on a period of probation and were expected to follow a course of training by reading certain books. On his travels he kept a check on them and as various Societies developed up and down the country he commended or reprimanded them as he felt necessary. At first he did his utmost to prevent any of the preachers from doing or saying anything which would cause the authorities to judge them as Dissenters. Later, whenever chapels were built the deed drawn up was done in such a way that it gave him the sole right to make any preaching appointment there, so that the Society would not fall into the hands of any who preached other doctrines. Up to the time of Jane's death there was no such thing as a preacher's allowance and they were forbidden by Wesley to accept cash from anybody. They could receive gifts of kind such as food and lodgings as they carried out their preaching duties, but this varied from place to place and depended on the generosity of the people to whom they preached, some of whom were in poor circumstances. As the saying goes, "they preached for their bacon". Some of them were fortunate in being provided with a horse, but if not they would have to provide one themselves and bear the expense of its upkeep or walk round the Circuit. For those who were married the difficulties were multiplied, especially when the preacher was away for longer periods. Later when it was felt necessary to agree some allowance for the preacher and his family, depending on which Circuit he was placed, it could not always be met, for often the 'class money' contribution from each Society fell short of what was required to run the Circuit. Apart from the financial hardship which the preacher had to put up with there was also the physical hardship of having to travel in all kinds of weather over many miles of track and road, where perhaps at the end of the journey they had to meet with opposition from those who did not favour their brand of Christianity. Not all of them gave a life's service in this way - some gave up altogether and were spiritually lost, whilst others were physically unable to carry out their duties any longer, but yet kept their faith and served locally whenever they could. It was to those preachers, however, whose minds and spirits and bodies did not flinch as they travelled about the country preaching and giving of their service that Methodism owes a great debt. They accepted whatever came their way and the poverty which they endured and the obedience which they gave were a natural consequence of their service. (14)

The first Quarterly Meeting to be held in Methodism went ahead as planned, when the leaders from five Societies met at the house of Mr. Major Marshall at Todmorden Edge on 18th October 1748, thus initiating a practice which was to continue until the 1970's, functioning as the main administrative meeting in a Methodist Circuit.

Bennet informed Wesley in a letter sent to him on 22nd October about the events at that first meeting, part of which read, "Four stewards were appointed to inspect into, and regulate the temporal affairs of the Societies; every leader brought his class paper and showed what money he had received that Quarter, which was fairly entered in a book for that purpose. The several Bills of Charge were brought in at the same and after

24

they were thoroughly examined were all discharged. But alas! the people are exceeding poor and will not be able to maintain the preachers and William Darney's family. The overplus after the Bills were discharged was only 9/2. ....Oh dear Sir let this method be used in other places. Once a year we propose to meet all the leaders and at other Quarterly Meetings the Stewards in each respective Society need only to be present with the particular accounts. I have made a small book which I have kept in the Box with the accounts, wherein an exact account of the Marriages, Deaths, Backsliders etc., shall be noted down that I may be able to give you an account thereof each Quarter".
(15)

Thankfully the account book which he refers to and which he kept 'in the Box' still survives and provides information which gives a clearer understanding of Methodism in the vicinity about Todmorden and East Lancashire in those early years. Each quarters accounts are recorded on facing pages, the left hand side showing the income and the right hand the expenditure, with a breakdown giving separate amounts for each Society. On a fly leaf is a Minute regarding the election of Stewards and a Memorandum stating what should be done in case of a dispute. The first five quarters from the October 1748 meeting, up to and including the October meeting the following year, are all set out in a similar manner, but then the records cease for almost five years, after which they are renewed in a different format giving less information but covering a wider geographical area. This book has come to be regarded as the Haworth Circuit Book. (16)

According to Dr. Frank Baker, Haworth was separated from the Cheshire Round and from the Leeds and Birstal Rounds in 1748/49. The boundaries of some of the Circuits at this time are not easy to delineate from the evidence that is available, and if they are known it cannot be assumed that they remained fixed year after year. The contents of the Haworth Circuit Book have been examined and written about by a number of writers of Methodist history, who have regarded the material found in the book as a continuing record, despite the five year gap, of the development of the Haworth Circuit from its earliest beginnings under the leadership of Rev. William Grimshaw. (17) From this assumption it has also been regarded that he was the Chairman of the first Quarterly Meeting. But did the Societies which met at Todmorden Edge on that October day, and which has been noted were former Darney Societies, form part of a Circuit centred on Haworth, and was Grimshaw even present at the Meeting?

His presence has always been presumed because the writing up of the first quarterly accounts, which are headed 'Todmorden Edge Accounts', has been attributed to him; whereas the handwriting actually belongs to John Bennet, and this can easily be confirmed by making a comparison with the writing in his Diary. It is more than likely therefore that Darney's former Societies were part of John Bennet's jurisdiction from Cheshire, which according to the Conference Minutes already noted covered Lancashire. The Quarterly Meeting which was held two days after the Todmorden meeting was

July 11. 1729   Cash rec.   £   s   d

Societies.	Leaders Names.	Cash		Bro. over 23. 10. 10		
Todmorden	Saml. Greenwood	4	11			
	Elias Crowther	7	9			
	John Eastwood	4	5			
	Robt. Ridman	4	10	Tot.	1	9	1
	John Marshall Ji:	4	11			
	John Marshall	2	3			
Heppenstall	John Fielding	4	4			
	John Barker	5	3			
	John Dearden	7	4			
	Robt. Shuttleworth					
	Wm. Farrar	2	1			
	John Coates	0	4	Tot	2	4	2
	Wm. Parker	0	2			
	John Coffey	5	5			
	Grace Spencer	3	2			
Rough Lee	Alice Dyson	2	6			
	Bernard Dyson	0	9			
	Saml. Varley	4	9			
	Edwd. Holt	7	3	Tot	1	13	8
Higham	Tho. Lowcock	1	4			
Padiam &c	Tho. Asden	4	2			
Lodge	James Hunter	4	11			
Goodshaw	Jno. Butterworth	0	8			
Chappels	Jas. Helliwell	6	0	Tot		15	4
Rosindale	John Hoyle	4	2			
	Saml. Gilliag	2	10			
	John Maden sen	3	5			
	John Maden	2	7	Tot	1	4	8
	Geo. Taylor	2	6			
	Geo. Ramsbottom	4	11			
	James Nuttal	4	3			
Midgley	Rich. Taylor	0	0	Tot		10	8
	Do.	1	7			
		31	0	0		

Facsimile page of the Haworth Circuit Record Book.
(*Reproduced with the permission of Keighley Reference Library*)

26

comprised of the leaders from the Societies situated in South Lancashire, Cheshire and Derbyshire. Thus the two meetings would cover practically all of the Cheshire Circuit. Sheffield and Nottingham were the only Societies not included, but it is even doubtful if the latter place stayed part of the Cheshire Circuit, for whilst there are various times in his Diary that Bennet records visiting Sheffield, not once does he make reference of going to Nottingham in the year following the 1748 Conference.

As to whether Grimshaw was at the first meeting it is difficult to determine. It has been recorded that there were thirty people present, apart from the host Mr. Marshall, based on the entry of a 5/- charge to cover the cost of the dinners at two pence per head. (18) The number arrived at was made up of the twenty seven leaders, plus Grimshaw, Bennet and Darney. The figure of twenty seven was determined because although there were twenty nine classes represented the names of William Parker and John Madin each appear as leaders of two classes. A closer look at subsequent entries, however, indicates that there were two John Madins - Senior and Junior. So in all probability there were twenty eight leaders present. Furthermore, James Dyson, who was elected steward along with James Greenwood, John Parker, and John Madin, is not listed as a Class Leader, but it is unlikely that he would have been chosen if he had not been present at the meeting. With Bennet obviously there this would bring the number up to thirty, but it should not be construed as definitive evidence of the composition of the meeting, for this would leave Darney unaccounted for.

Bennet's Diary contains entries relating to each of the first four Quarterly Meetings which were held at Todmorden and it is interesting to note that on the first occasion there is no reference to any other party being there, but for the following three meetings the names of the preachers who were present are given, with William Grimshaw being included in the last two. (19) This again cannot be regarded as conclusive evidence as to who was at the first meeting, since the omission of a name does not preclude one from being there, but it does give further cause to question a long held assumption.

That the Haworth cleric was at the fifth and last of these early meetings held in October 1749 cannot be in doubt, for the accounts are written up in Grimshaw's hand, with the whereabouts of John Bennet unknown, he having failed to write up his Diary for several weeks. Personal circumstances had somewhat changed for him, because earlier that month he had married Grace Murray, with whom John Wesley thought he had an understanding. Before the marriage the emotional entanglements involving the three parties had placed a strain on the personal relationships of Bennet and Wesley. This became particularly acute because of the quickly arranged marriage, although Bennet was not the motivator. The culprit was Charles Wesley, who did not consider Grace suitable for his brother, and believing that such a marriage might also make John's leadership less effective he moved quickly. Whilst John was preaching in Cumbria, Charles headed north. Calling for Grace on the way she was persuaded to accompany him to Newcastle, where the marriage ceremony took place, with Charles and also Whitefield acting as witnesses.

Some form of reconciliation took place between the two men shortly after the marriage and Bennet continued his duties as one of Wesley's Assistants, with his work now concentrated in the Cheshire, Derbyshire and South Lancashire area as far north as Bolton and Rochdale. It was probably from this time that the former Darney Societies began to be administered by Grimshaw, and formed part of the Haworth Circuit.

Facsimile page from John Bennet's Diary
(Reproduced from the collections of the Methodist Archives and Research Centre, the John Rylands University Library of Manchester)

Chapter Four

New Territory

Several months before the first Quarterly Meeting was held a completely different part of Lancashire began to be evangelized and it was because of a connection with Rossendale that Methodism suddenly took this fresh leap into new territory. The initiator of the move was Thomas Butterworth of Shorrocks Green, whose kinsfolk lived at Goodshaw, but once again Bennet was the means by which Methodism spread to the new area. Thomas appears to have been the father of Henry Butterworth, described as a pious blacksmith of Goodshaw, who lived there with his large family. (1) Goodshaw was a stronghold of the Baptist cause, and four of Henry's sons were later to become ministers of that denomination in various parts of the country, but before that at least one of them, John, had espoused Methodism. 'Everett' informs us that John had heard Wesley when he preached at Newchurch in Rossendale, and also John Nelson, before becoming a regular attender at the Methodist meetings. (2) Most likely it was he who was one of the two class leaders from Goodshaw who attended the four Quarterly Meetings held in 1749 and whose name is so recorded in the Account Book. It was a year or so before this that his grandfather Thomas had invited Bennet to preach at Shorrocks Green.

Bennet, however, was not the first nonconformist preacher to visit the area. Some years earlier David Crossley, the Baptist minister from Bacup, before his death in 1744 had made periodic preaching visits to Shorrocks Green, but nothing permanent was established. (3) Because of the strong connection that the Butterworth family had with the Baptists it seems likely that this was at the instigation of Thomas Butterworth.

At the end of 1747 Bennet was on a preaching tour of East Lancashire, but three days into the new year, after preaching at Miller Barn, he headed west accompanied by several members of the Rossendale Society to a place which he described as "...about three miles behind Blackburn". He continued, "We got to the place appointed in due time... I was in the midst of the Papist and amongst a people that had never heard of the Methodists. They looked upon me as if I brought them some new Doctrine". After preaching to them he arranged to speak again in the evening, but thought that not many would attend. Instead the house was full. That night he stayed at Shorrocks Green and the following morning, before leaving for Bolton, he met several people who had come from some nearby community who asked him "to come over and help them". (4)

Shorrocks Green does not exist as a village today, but its whereabouts can be determined since it appears on Yates's map of Lancashire and from which it is evident that there were a number of dwellings in the locality. It is shown in the south west part of Mellor to the east of Samlesbury Bottoms, near to the entrance of the later Woodfold Hall. Today there is just a narrow country road with an occasional farm or house.

Bennet's Diary gives no indication as to where those people who visited him that morning at Shorrocks Green came from, but it seems that they must have come from the Hoghton side of the River Darwen, which was easily fordable. The manner in which they asked him to "come over" could be construed as being to somewhere on the other side of the river, but more conclusive is the fact that when Bennet next came on a preaching visit to Shorrocks Green four weeks later he also made a planned stop at Ollerton in Withnell, not too far from Hoghton Tower.

On this second visit to Thomas Butterworth's he once again stayed overnight, preached twice, found time to spend an hour at the Nab's Head Inn in conversation with an old beggarman bookseller and visit a sick woman. Yet again whilst staying here he received a deputation of several men, who asked him to give them a sermon sometime in the future at Hoghton Tower. Sir Henry Hoghton normally retained a Dissenting Minister at the Tower, who was obliged to preach at the chapel there to those who lived and worked in the vicinity, but he had left and because a replacement was not due to arrive until May Bennet promised that if it was possible he would arrange to visit them in the future. On his way over to his appointment at Ollerton he did call at the chapel, where they were able to sing a couple of verses of a hymn, but that was all, for to do anything more at that time would have been too presumptuous. It is interesting to note that Bennet recorded that the Tower was "an old spacious building, but much run to decay". His preaching appointment at Ollerton was at the house of John Edge, described as being near to Lockwood Smithy, where his message was well received. (5)

It was six months before Bennet was in the vicinity again, some two weeks after John Jane's release from Preston. The visit was probably made in connection with Jane's pending case, for besides preaching at Shorrocks Green, he called on Richard Whitehead, JP and then went to Preston, where he called at the House of Correction. He was warmly received by the Governor and his family, who had been spiritually influenced by Bennet on the earlier visit. The preacher records that he had business to do in the town, so he left his horse at the prison and set about his task, accompanied by the Governor who would not leave his side for a moment. It seems that James Stanley and his family must have been the first in the town to have been influenced by a visiting Methodist preacher. Later that day, on his way to Bolton, Bennet called at a place known as Brimmicroft, near Hoghton Tower, and preached at the home of William Fazackerly, where he spent the night. (6)

The area to the west of Blackburn was new ground for the Methodists and the

WESLEYAN METHODIST CHAPEL ERECTED 1794.

Date Stone - Hoghton Chapel

Hoghton Methodist Chapel

EW

ventures at Shorrocks Green and Brimmicroft were the beginnings of what was to become a slow but gradual Methodist influence in this rural part of Lancashire, long before it was established in the town of Blackburn. Whilst documentary evidence of Methodist activity in this district is spasmodic prior to the setting up of Blackburn as the head of a new Circuit in 1787, there can be no doubt that there has been continuity of support for the Methodist cause from its earliest days here. Even though Shorrocks Green and Brimmicroft have long since passed into Methodist history, their subsequent successor at Hoghton, midway between these two early preaching places, still continues to this day and the chapel built there in 1794 is the oldest original chapel in the present North Lancashire District.

At the present time Brimmicroft lies just to the west of the Hoghton to Belmont road, not far from the Leeds and Liverpool Canal. Besides the original farmstead, now converted, the small community consists of a handful of houses. Access to it is over an unpaved lane. Most people who travel along the nearby main road will pass the place with hardly a glance, and even the Methodists amongst them probably do not know of its earlier significance.

One of Darney's pieces of doggerel made reference to the place when he wrote:-
"At Sherfanside and Brimmicroft, the work it is begun
And Satan's soldiers they do fight, for fear we take Blackburn". (7)

Bennet made further preaching visits to this area later in 1748, one of the occasions being when the Quarter Session hearing was held. He was also here again in the following year, (8) but as already indicated, towards the end of the decade his work was concentrated more in the Cheshire Circuit nearer his Chinley home. In addition his Diary becomes more spasmodic about this time and does not reveal any further evidence of his coming to these parts. The work that had been started, however, continued and in January 1751 the Quarter Sessions held that month in Preston reveal that John Edge and William Anderton petitioned for the house of William Fazackerly to be registered as a meeting place for protestant dissenters, thus indicating that they were still anticipating visits from the travelling preachers. (9)

Up to about 1750 Wesley had encouraged the avoidance of having to obtain a licence for any place used as a preaching house, in the belief that if it was done those people meeting there would be regarded as Dissenters, which he wanted to avoid at all costs. From after this date, however, many of the places began to be registered despite the fact that the term 'protestant dissenters' was often used in the application, as it was then felt that it would not deny members their standing in the Established Church. This newer interpretation made matters more confusing and it remained so throughout most of the century, with even local magistrates being put in doubt as to how to apply the Acts governing registration. (10)

Although Brimmicroft could be classified as a Bennet inspired Society rather than a Darney one it is obvious from the latter's composition of verse that he was familiar with the area. Now that Bennet was concentrating his efforts elsewhere, additional support for the new venture could be expected to come from the preachers attached to the Haworth Circuit, with perhaps an occasional visit from Grimshaw himself, who was now travelling extensively amongst the Methodist Societies in the northern counties, especially considering that his family home was at nearby Brindle.

Unfortunately, just prior to the work becoming established in these parts, elsewhere in the east part of Lancashire, Methodism went into decline. Some of the leaders as well as ordinary members were lost from the cause and in turn this affected the newly won area west of Blackburn.

The first intimation of the reverse was the failure of the Quarterly Meeting, with the one that was due to be held in January 1750 not taking place. It has already been mentioned that there was a gap of five years in the Account Book, which had this comment placed in it by way of explanation:- "Whereas it appears from this Book that no Accounts are therein inserted from October 31st 1749 to this present Day July 25th 1754 - Be it known that the Reason of it is the Discontinuing Quarter Meetings from that to this Day".

In attempting to explain the abandonment of these meetings it is necessary to take a closer look at William Darney. Right from the beginning of his preaching about Birstal it was clear that his message, which was given in a Calvinistic vein, raised some objections in the mind of John Nelson, with whom he was then sometimes associated. Nelson followed the doctrine of John Wesley, who was not a believer of predestination, but who nevertheless did not object to any of his preachers from holding such views so long as they kept them to themselves and did not introduce this doctrine into their preaching. Whenever they did Wesley was quick to act. Darney was unorthodox and not particularly well educated, although he seems to have had a charisma about him by which he was able to establish a following. Concerning this George Whitefield was able to write "...though seemingly unqualified...many date their awakening..hearing him". (11) When Darney became a travelling preacher the discipline and strictures which went with the work appear to have sometimes conflicted with his freedom of spirit, and it was this spirit which led him to compose several hymns, many of which were unusual or simply just doggerel, and then using them at his preaching services to the annoyance of Wesley. Much to the dismay of Darney the lack of discipline he displayed resulted in Wesley removing him from his Connexion at the beginning of 1750, which thus precluded him from preaching in any of Wesley's Societies. (12)

Quite naturally this in turn upset some of the Darney followers, but even in this respect Wesley let it be known that the choice of whether they wished to remain in the

Methodist Connexion was up to each Society concerned and then only if they could put themselves in some order.

The state of these Societies was brought to the attention of John Bennet whilst he was visiting Rochdale towards the end of January that year, when several brethren sought help and advice from him, because of the disruptions that had occurred amongst them. The following day he went to Miller Barn and attempted to bring a spirit of unity to the Society, having found some of them deeply prejudiced. It was the same at Todmorden Edge, which he visited, where most of the members were embittered towards Darney, who Bennet had not yet seen. Very soon, however, he was able to speak with him privately and learn about Wesley's displeasure which had resulted in his removal from the band of preachers. (13) Concern for the distraught Societies caused Wesley to correspond with Bennet and William Shent, a leader of the Society at Leeds, near to where Darney had his home. As a result it was decided that a lengthy period of supervision would be needed before order could be restored over the unsettled Societies, but since Bennet did not have the time to spare Wesley felt that the only thing that could be done was for John Nelson and the other Yorkshire preachers to visit them whenever they could. Grimshaw, who apparently took Darney under his wing again, was also appraised of the situation.

The amount of disruption that the old Darney Societies suffered varied from place to place, but most of them were able to carry on, though not as effectively as before and sometimes with a change of location. The abandonment of the Quarterly Meeting did not mean that all the leaders of the various classes forsook their duties, but it did mean that the administrative control was curtailed for a time, with some losses being suffered as a result. Within Lancashire a few of the former leaders kept the spirit alive locally; men such as James Varley from Roughlee, James Hunter from Padiham, Major Marshall from Todmorden and George Ramsbottom from the Haslingden class belonging to the Rossendale Society. (14) After his visit to Roughlee and Miller Barn in June 1752, (15) Wesley did not visit either North East Lancashire or Rossendale for a further five years, except to preach once at Newhall Hey, south of Haslingden. (16) In Rossendale the cause was as good as lost, but thankfully at Bacup there was one man, John Madin, who kept the embers aglow when all the other members had deserted to follow different paths, (17) and it was to be 1757 before the Society was re-established there. During this period if Madin wanted to meet with other fellow Methodists he would have had to travel outside his immediate area to satisfy his needs, and it is possible that some of the traditions surrounding his visits to Gauxholme may be attributable to this period. In October 1756 when Charles Wesley was at Gauxholme there were a number of Baptists who listened to his preaching, which prompted James Allen to inform him "they have carried off no less than fifty out of one Society,....several Baptist meetings are wholly made out of old Methodists". (18) Could one of these places have been John Madin's Society? The Circuit records which were recommended by

Grimshaw in 1754 reveal evidence of the disruption. Whilst Roughlee and Todmorden survived as centres of Lancashire Methodism they did so at first with a reduced membership. Besides Bacup, the former Miller Barn and Goodshaw Societies are not even mentioned; the only exception being George Ramsbottom's class, which was able to develop and become the spearhead of the cause at Haslingden.

In this early era of Methodism, when it was not always easy to hold preaching services at a regular place, the names of the Societies were subject to change. The classes were sometimes in a state of flux as a result of having to depend on the goodwill and faithfulness of the people involved in providing accommodation. Sometimes the blossoming of, or the failure of a class, or the change of residence of a leader or dominant person often led to a change in the Society's name. By 1755 Major Marshall had moved from Todmorden Edge and had gone to live at Stansfield, further away on the other side of the Calder Valley, [19] and so his home which had been used to house those early Quarterly Meetings was no longer available for the Methodists, and it was from this point that Gauxholme became the focus of the cause. It may have been Gauxholme that John Wesley was referring to when he visited the area in April that year and preached to the people who "...stood, row above row, on the side of the mountain". [20] It certainly fits the description.

How much the new found Society at Brimmicroft suffered as a result of the disruption in the eastern part of Lancashire has not been recorded, nor is it known for certain under whose preaching jurisdiction it came whilst the Quarterly Meetings were not being held. Even if Bennet did make an occasional visit to the area whenever he was around Bolton this would not last long because of his disagreement and break with Wesley in 1752. Sometime during the following four years one of those Society name changes took place at Brimmicroft, and by inference also its meeting place. The move was but a short distance away; to a small fold known as Laund, half a mile to the south west. It was to this Laund that William Grimshaw came in June 1756. During the second week of the month he set out on a preaching tour, and after spending the first night at Bentley Wood Green he called at Feniscowles in the township of Livesey, where there had been some recent Presbyterian influence. [21]

Later the same day he travelled a further two miles to Laund, where he was able to meet with the members and preach to them. After spending the night there he preached again the following morning before going to visit his mother close by at Marsh Lane, Brindle, where he lived as a boy. [22]

One of the most essential requirements for maintaining a Society in its formative years was the dedicated men and women who had sufficient strength of faith and character to hold fast to their beliefs between the itinerant preachers visits and help maintain the fellowship which had been created. What administrative records there are cannot reveal the difficulties that some of these people had to endure. Whilst they did not always have to contend with physical violence, there is no doubt that they had to withstand much ridicule and aggravation which often led to a feeling of isolation, especially if the visits from the preachers were few and far between. That Methodism was able to survive in the rural area south west of Blackburn throughout this period was because of a few such faithful people.

In 1758 the Society at Laund Fold began to support the Haworth Circuit financially and the records show that their contributions were taken to the Quarterly Meetings by two of the local preachers in the Circuit, James Crossley of Heptonstall and William Parker of Wadsworth. Subsequently they were generally taken by the travelling preachers as they were doing their rounds, except on two occasions when the journey was made by two of the leaders; George Ainsworth, a farmer of Brimmicroft and John Grime, a weaver. (23)

From now on the movement in the county began to expand and the prejudice which had been fermented by Rev. George White at Colne had sufficiently died down for a Society to be started there. It soon became the dominant Society in North East Lancashire and was destined to become the head of a new Circuit. Other Lancashire Societies contributing to the Haworth Circuit about this time not already mentioned were Top o'th Coal Pits, Facit, Bank House near Rochdale, Dunnockshaw, Darwen and one known as Old Paper Mill. By the start of 1763 expansion was taking place into the dales of north west Yorkshire and as far away as Kendal and Lupton in what is now Cumbria. Unfortunately William Grimshaw, who had travelled and toiled so extensively for the cause of Evangelism and Methodism throughout the Haworth Circuit and beyond did not live to see the development of this new 'Forest Round', which later in the year, together with the other Yorkshire and Lancashire Societies, helped to make the Circuit one of the most extensive in Methodism. (24) William who died in the April of that year was one of only a few who were able to play a leading role in nurturing the Methodist cause, whilst still maintaining a successful parish ministry. Despite his untimely death this large Circuit came to be known as Grimshaw's Great Haworth Round.

❖

Chapter Five

Progress in Preston and Colne

At the Conference following Grimshaw's death it was decided to make Keighley the administrative centre for the Circuit, although for a further few years it was still referred to as the Haworth Circuit. In terms of size Keighley was the logical choice, but Haworth had retained the pre-eminence up to this time because of the leadership of Grimshaw. Resulting from the change a new Circuit book was started and contained amongst its early entries are lists of members for all the Lancashire Societies except Colne. (1)

At Brimmicroft, which in 1763 had once more become the name of the Society in that area, the membership totalled thirty eight, twenty of whom were men. It was divided into two classes with some of the members coming from Hoghton, Ollerton and Livesey. The majority were either spinners or weavers; but two were farmers, one a miller and another a carpenter. Earlier than this, in 1762, a Methodist Meeting House had been established at Preston in a barn belonging to Roger Fishwick, a chapman; but it does not seem to have fostered any permanent class or society in the town at that time. (2) In neighbouring Walton le Dale there was more success. By the beginning of that year a nucleus had gathered themselves together, probably as a result of some influence from the Laund or Ollerton area, to form a small Society, which became part of the Haworth Circuit. On the same day that the petition for the Preston meeting place was made, the same petitioners, Thomas Morton of Preston, William Hollinhurst and Richard Cartwright, both of Walton, also requested that the latter's home at Cockshut House, on the main road between Walton and Bamber Bridge, be likewise registered. (3) The membership lists show that there was just one class of seventeen members, led by William Livesey. Amongst this number were three people who lived in Preston; James Thompson and his wife Margaret, and a Miss Martha Thompson.

The life of Martha Thompson has been recorded on several previous occasions, and she has been sung and spoken about in musical and dramatic productions. She has been acclaimed as the first Methodist in Preston and instrumental in helping create the first Society in the town. Her name has long been associated with the development of Methodism as it gained ground, but it should not be overlooked that there were also others, whose exploits are less well documented who played their part.

Martha and her twin brother, John, were born to Henry and Ann Thompson of Preston in 1733 and baptized at St. John's Parish Church, (4) but when they were only a few years old their mother died. Eventually Henry remarried, but because of difficulties which later developed with her step-mother Martha left home when she was in her late teens

To the Worshipful his Majestys Justices of the peace Assembled at the General Quarter Sessions of the peace at Preston in and for the County of Lancaster the 22 Day of April 1762—

We whose names are hereunder subscribed Do hereby petition and request you to Record the Born and Authored... Dragon Fishwick in Preston aforesaid (Lapwire to be a Meeting house for a sett of persons being Dissenters from the Church of England to Exercise their Religious Worship in Witness our hands—

Thos Morton
Willm Hollinhurst
Richard Cartwright

Facsimile petition for the registration of a (Methodist) Meeting House in Preston.
(Original at the Lancashire Record Office Ref. QSP1824/20.
Crown Copyright. Reproduced with the permission of the Controller of Her Majesty's Stationery Office).

to work as a domestic in London for a former Preston lady. After having been thus employed for a few years she had reason to pass through Moorfields one day whilst on an errand for her mistress, when she was attracted by a motley throng which had burst into song. Intrigued, she stopped and listened, and when the singing had finished she stayed on to listen to the preacher who had climbed on a table to speak. He wore a clergyman's gown and bands, and spoke with such authority that Martha's conscience was aroused and she stood riveted to the spot for twenty minutes or more. The preacher was non other than John Wesley. On her return she explained to her mistress the reason for her delay and described how the words of Wesley had made an impression on her. Her mistress, however, was distressed at the news and believing it was her duty as a good churchwoman she advised Martha not to go to listen to the Methodists again; but Martha's conscience had been disturbed and she felt a sense of guilt which bothered her so much that she returned some time later to Moorfields, and whilst there was converted. During the singing of the last hymn it is recorded that with tears in her eyes her sense of guilt was removed and replaced with joy and gladness. Her religious experience was such that she felt that she had to share it with others, but apparently her enthusiasm became too much for her fellow workers, who convinced their mistress that Martha was going mad. As a result a doctor was called for who pronounced her insane and had her committed to the asylum at Bedlam.

Whilst there she suffered the indignities which all the inmates had to endure; her hair was cut, her head shaved, she was harshly treated and made to feel an outcast of society. Fortunately her spirit remained resolute and her new found confidence in God stood her in good stead. Gradually she was able to find favour with her keepers, who found her responsible enough to employ her with needle and thread, later to be followed by work in the kitchens. Having no friends or relatives in London she did not have anyone to visit her until eventually she had the opportunity to talk with a man when he came to visit his wife. On one of these occasions she found that he too was a Methodist, so enlisting his help she arranged for him to take a letter which she had written to John Wesley. Within a few days Wesley had negotiated her freedom and then had her cared for pending one of his preaching tours, when he planned to get her home. This was accomplished shortly afterwards and Martha found herself riding pillion behind Wesley as he headed northwards. She travelled with him as far as the Midlands, where a cart was found that was eventually to bring her to Lancashire, and then on home to Preston and to those whom she knew. Soon she was at work as a mantle maker and milliner. (5)

It is not known where Martha worshipped on her return home, but she did listen for news of the Methodists, and especially for any preaching or meeting that was to occur nearby. At this point of her life it is recorded that she began to make the journey of six miles to Brimmicroft on foot, but the Circuit records show that, between April 1758 up to the time that the Walton Society commenced, the Society was centred on Laund or

Ollerton. (6) The life of the Walton Society only seems to have been of short duration, for following the summer of 1765 it ceased to make contributions to the Circuit, and it does not reappear in the records until over twenty years later. Possibly Martha may have had an association with Brimmicroft at this time. In Preston Roger Fishwick and Thomas Morton still had an allegiance with Methodism and soon Martha's life became centred more in this direction. This was because of another association which had developed, and which resulted in her being married at St. John's to Joseph Whitehead in November 1766. (7) Soon children followed, at least three of whom survived to adulthood; Nancy, John and Joseph. Joseph, Senior, was a successful button manufacturer and brass founder. They lived just to the west of the Parish Church, behind the buildings forming the south side of Church Street, in an area which at that time was mainly open space with few houses but a number of garden plots. Following the growth of the factory based cotton industry in subsequent years this space was quickly filled with tenement houses and a labyrinth of alleyways and wiends and the character of the area changed. Nevertheless the Whiteheads remained here in what became known as Turks Head Court and where John Horrocks developed his cotton mill. Resulting from this a close friendship grew between the two families, until eventually they became united with the marriage of John Whitehead and Mary Horrocks, sister of John.

The beginning of a new home and the start of a family concentrated more of Martha's efforts to the fostering of Methodism in Preston and in 1769 a request was made to the Haworth Circuit for one of the travelling preachers to visit the town, which culminated in a visit during the first half of that year. The preacher who came was Thomas Mitchell, and is reported to have spoken outdoors, but whether he was successful in persuading any of his hearers to follow the Methodist way of life is unknown. However, his presence was noted by some, for during the night he was taken from his bed by assailants and dumped in a pond before being left somewhere on the outskirts of the town. (8)

The suspicion that there may have been some form of Methodist fellowship in Preston was given further credence when Joseph Whitehead joined with Fishwick and Morton in giving support to work that had been started at Mellor. Surely these Preston men would hardly give support to work outside the town if they had not already formed some kind of a group within its boundaries. At Mellor the influence was Thomas Cowpe, and during the summer of 1770 the four of them were instrumental in obtaining the disused Mellor windmill as a meeting place for the Methodists. (9) In that same summer there was also some realignment of the Haworth Circuit. Bewersal at Rochdale became part of the Manchester Circuit and a new Society was formed a few miles north of the town at Dobbin, which probably also incorporated members from nearby Facit. (10) At the same time the Circuit ceased to be responsible for the most westerly of its Lancashire Societies. Only two were shown in the records; Top o' Coal Pits and Brimmicroft, and these were transferred to the Liverpool Circuit. (11) On the changeover the latter Society relocated its meeting place and became known as Moulding Water; a place still in the township of Hoghton, but about a mile to the east of Brimmicroft. How this change affected those who were connected with Methodism in Preston and Mellor is not clear, for it is not known which Circuit was responsible for their pastoral care. Especially as there was still no Methodist influence evident in Blackburn, their links with Haworth would have been lessened because of the realignment, but if they had now come under the jurisdiction of the Liverpool Circuit they would still be on the periphery of things.

Within a few more years the band of followers at Preston began to feel a little more optimistic about their future when they found a new meeting place. From the early days Martha Whitehead had been taking one of her neighbours with her whenever she attended the Methodist meetings. She was Isabel Walmsley, a widow who ran the Dog Inn on Church Street, supported by her son William, who also had become a Methodist. Eventually after having been part of the group for some time Isabel allowed the Methodists to use the Dog Inn as their meeting place. (12) From 1774 it became the centre of the growing cause in the town and was used as the preaching place to which the travelling preachers increasingly came, culminating in the visit in 1780 of John Wesley himself.

Following the Methodist Conference of 1776 the Haworth Circuit was split and from it the new more compact Colne Circuit was created, to which two preachers were appointed to serve for one year; 'Sammy' Bardsley and William Brammah. 'Sammy' was another one of those men who, though uneducated, was dedicated to preaching the gospel whenever and wherever he could, and this included the streets of Preston, which formed part of the new Circuit. His limited acquaintance with English grammar and a slight speech impediment resulted in him sometimes being ridiculed when he preached outdoors, but with his wit and common sense and his undoubted knowledge of the bible many of his interrupters were silenced and some were converted. His preaching was convincing enough to influence Roger Crane, a young man of nineteen, in becoming a member of the Preston Society during his time in the Circuit. (13)

The Crane family had lived in the vicinity of Preston and Chorley for over two hundred years, with most of them tending to support Nonconformity in general and Presbyterianism in particular. One branch of the family settled at Penwortham in the early part of the 18th Century and their home was used as a Dissenting Preaching House, whilst Roger's uncle Edward was at one time the minister of the famous Octagon Chapel at Norwich, a building much admired by John Wesley and whose style was copied when some of the first Methodist chapels were built. Roger's father Thomas was in the ironmongery business and following the death of his younger brother Samuel, as a result of injuries received in an election riot in 1767, Thomas amalgamated his business with that of his bereaved sister in law. As a result the family became comparatively well off and they too held a respectable social position in town. As soon as he was capable Roger assisted his father in the business, his mother having died when he was about two years old. (14)

The Presbyterian church in Preston, which the family attended, became a centre of controversy when the minister began to espouse a Unitarian doctrine and he was successful in persuading some of his Trustees to follow the same path. Although those who had more orthodox Presbyterian views, including the Cranes, tried to prevent this faction from taking over they were unsuccessful and the church became Unitarian, resulting in Thomas and his family looking elsewhere to satisfy their spiritual needs. Whilst they were still looking, Roger and his father happened to be in Leeds on one occasion where they heard one of Wesley's preachers, but nothing which they heard persuaded them to join the Methodists. That was until Roger heard 'Sammy' Bardsley, who over a period of a few weeks counselled him and guided his thoughts until one day he committed himself and became a member of the Preston Society. At first he expected his father to show some displeasure or opposition when he started to attend the Methodist meetings, but on the contrary he received his father's full approbation and shortly afterwards his older twin sisters, Mary and Elizabeth, joined the Society. Consequently the family home became a place of welcome and hospitality for all the travelling preachers who visited the town. The personal qualities and energies which the Cranes contributed to the Preston Society in its formative years and in wider Methodism later were of great value and their influence touched the lives of many with whom they came in contact, helping to bring them a deeper faith.

About the same time as the Cranes joined the Preston Society another young man, Michael Emmet, became a member of that group. (15) He was the eldest son of the large family of Michael Sr., who ran the hostelry known as 'The Ram's Head' in the vicinity of Gin Bow Entry, off Market Place. When he was in his early teens young Michael became apprenticed to a cabinet maker and upholsterer, and during his time in service he met up with William Walmsley, who persuaded him to attend the Methodist meetings at the Dog Inn. Through this Michael began to read the bible more regularly and eventually committed himself to a Christian life in association with the other Methodists, but in the course of doing so alienated himself from his father, who turned him out of the family home. Fortunately he was then able to earn his own living as a cabinet maker and joiner. Soon after his conversion he formed a lasting friendship with Roger Crane and was a regular visitor to his home, becoming almost part of the family. On these visits, of course, he also met Roger's sisters and before long a relationship had commenced with Mary, which eventually led to him joining the family in 1781 when they were married at St. John's. (16)

Whilst Roger and Michael were developing their friendship there was another young man in Preston who was seeking a purpose to his life. He was William Bramwell, who

43

had been born into a large family at Elswick, who worshipped at the Established Church down the road at Copp. When he was growing up he attended the services regularly and sang in the choir from being a child, having a love of music. On reaching his teens he was apprenticed out as a currier and fellmonger to a Mr. Brandreth of Preston and whilst he served there he started to take a more serious interest in religion, and began seeking for something that up to then he had not found. For a while he tried Catholicism, but later returned to the Anglican Church and was prepared for confirmation, but he was still not content. During this time, however, he had not lost his love of singing, and whenever he could he went round the public houses of Preston, of which there were many, singing to the customers. In the course of his visits he eventually came to the Dog Inn, where he was persuaded to return for the visit of the next travelling preacher, Christopher Hopper. This was towards the end of 1779 and during the course of two other visits he struck up a friendship with Roger and Michael and became part of the group. A few months later William was there for John Wesley's first visit to the Preston Society on Friday, 28th April 1780, and later he was to record how he received a word of encouragement from him and then, that same evening, after spending much time in prayer and meditation he was converted. The recording of this experience is valuable, not only because it was an important time in William's life, but also because the record of the Preston visit has been omitted from Wesley's Journal. (17)

For the next five years these three men, Roger, Michael and William, who soon became Class Leaders and Local Preachers, worked together in the promotion of Methodism locally and also throughout much of the surrounding countryside, especially William who was now qualified as a journeyman currier. His income was only limited, but out of his earnings he was sometimes able to hire a horse to take him on his more distant trips, combining his work with his preaching, whilst on other occasions he would walk twenty miles or so in the course of one journey. He visited Grimsargh, Longridge, Ribchester and the other villages towards Clitheroe and Blackburn. He also preached at Salwick, Woodplumpton, Kirkham, Garstang, Poulton and most of the Fylde villages. He had to encounter various indignities at the hands of some of the more unruly elements of his congregations. He was opposed by his parents, he was thrown in the mud, bitten by dogs and attacked by ruffians. Long after his death one of the family heirlooms was the long staff, spiked with an iron, that he used on occasions to defend himself from the dogs. Despite these setbacks his evangelizing had an effect on the lives of some of his hearers living in the Fylde and elsewhere. One of these was Ann Cutler of Thornley. When Bramwell was on one of his preaching journeys to Ribchester and vicinity, where by 1785 there were at least three meeting houses - Ribchester, Dutton Lee & Alston - (18) Ann went to hear him and was converted when she was in her twenties. She was but a poor hand loom weaver with a scanty education and little ability, but though regarded as eccentric by many of the locals, she herself became an evangelist at a time when it was not favourably regarded for women to do this work by the early Methodists. She was noted for having a special talent in the use of prayer, and it was by this means that she was able to do her work of evangelism, and

The Dog Inn, Church Street, Preston

she became known as 'Praying Nanny', and sometimes accompanied Bramwell when he was preaching.

In 1781 the membership of the Preston Society had increased so much that the meetings which sometimes were held in private houses were becoming overcrowded, and to alleviate this a room was obtained over a packer's warehouse in what was then known as St. John's Street (later part of Tithebarn Street), and this was used over the next six years until the first chapel was built. It was in this room that Wesley preached that year when he made his second visit to the Society, at which time Roger Crane and his father extended him the hospitality of their home. (19) It was not only the more well known Methodists that Roger gave his attention but he also gave help to some of the poorer people of Preston and this known generosity stood him in good stead when he was once visiting Poulton. On that occasion he was preaching from the fish stones there when he was dragged from his temporary pulpit and bundled out of the Market Place by a group of men towards a neighbouring pond. The commotion attracted others, including a prizefighter, who on enquiring as to what had happened realized who the preacher was. Knowing of Roger's good reputation amongst the poor of Preston he barged his way to the front of the crowd and let the leaders of the mob know that they would have to deal with him if they laid another hand on the preacher. Apparently, his reputation as a fighter must have been sufficiently well known for them to desist and he was able to lead Roger away to safety. (20)

Like Roger, Michael Emmet did not have the same opportunities to travel as did Bramwell, save on special occasions, but about 1784 he took a week off work in order to go on a preaching journey. Saddling up a horse which had been lent to him he set off to the north of Preston, visiting Garstang, Scorton and Wyresdale, where it is reported that he had some success preaching in a farmhouse at Marshaw, before travelling on to Lancaster. When he was at Garstang it happened to be market day and as he preached from the obelisk in the Market Place there were quite a number of farmers from about the area who were present. The story is told that on completion of his message he was pleasantly surprised when a man known as 'Quaker' Jackson spoke kindly to him, thanked him for the message and then gave him half a guinea to pay for his tolls and the upkeep of his horse, telling him to keep on with the good work. (21) An early example of ecumenicity. No doubt later in the day when the farmers returned to their various homes the events of the day would soon be passed on to others.

Over a period of about five years these three were greatly responsible for spreading the gospel about Preston and the surrounding area, sowing the seeds that would later bear fruit in many of the places that they had visited. Bramwell especially had a way of winning people over and impressed his friend Roger so much that he suggested that he should consider the possibility of becoming one of Wesley's preachers on a full time basis. This suggestion was also mentioned to the members of the Preston Society and as a group they endorsed the idea. Bramwell, however, was undecided what to do and for a while he struggled with his thoughts and his conscience. He was now reasonably set up in business and was happy doing his evangelizing amongst the people he knew in the Fylde and about Preston. In addition he had become engaged to one of his converts, a Miss Ellen Byrom, a dressmaker in the town. He regarded preaching locally and preaching in the wider Methodism both as callings, so after many deliberations he did what he realised he should have done at first and that was pray about it. Tradition says that he spent about thirty six hours in a stone quarry near Preston, away from everyone in prayer and contemplation, before he felt that God had called him to become a travelling preacher. He offered himself to Wesley and at the Conference of 1786 he was appointed to the Circuit at Canterbury. Later that year he sold his business, bought a horse and saddle bags and set off on the long journey of 300 miles, most likely as the first of Wesley's preachers to have come from the Fylde. The following year he was back at Preston, where in August he married Ellen at St. John's, (22) but although he had been appointed to go to Lynn Circuit, because of family cares he stayed on at Preston for a year.

By the time Bramwell had returned to Preston, Colne Circuit had been in existence for eleven years, during which time there had been a substantial growth in the membership, but a number of problems had been encountered over the period. During the first year the Society at Colne was busy raising funds and completing its chapel at Colne Lane. Much of the money for the purchase of the land and also the building had come from across the Yorkshire border, from folk living in Thornton, Marton and Salterforth. (23) Circuit records show that the Trustees appointed were William Sagar and William Barker of Southfield, John Wood of Park, John Bracewell and John Barritt of Salterforth and Abraham Beanland. By June 1777 the chapel had been completed but when Wesley came to preach unfortunately the whole of one gallery which was crowded with people collapsed and although no lives were lost there were several who had broken limbs or other injuries. (24) This necessitated the Circuit having to find funds to cover the large expense of those who were hurt, as well as rebuilding the gallery and completing some other work. The burden of this fell to Bardley's successor, Alexander Mather (1777-79) who travelled extensively to raise monies for the 'Gallery Fund'. (25) The following year he also had to deal with a dispute in connection with the building of a preaching house at Padiham. This building was damaged on more than one occasion during erection but, after a few months of disputing, the matter was determined by informal arbitration. (26) When Thomas Hanson (1781-83) was there the number of Circuit preachers had increased to three, but he was soon in correspondence with Wesley suggesting that the Circuit should be divided or that a fourth preacher should be appointed. Wesley, whilst agreeing that the Circuit was a hard one in which to serve, discarded both suggestions, except for one occasion when he provided temporary help for a short while, due to the disaffection of David Evans (1782-83) who was contemplating leaving the itinerancy. (27)

Charles Atmore (1784-85) was in the Circuit for two years, first as the third preacher but then as senior. His memoirs record that on entering the Circuit he was oppressed by the state of the Societies and the smallness of the congregations, but during his term he saw an improvement in every part of it except north of Pendle Hill. He made special reference to the Societies of Blackburn and neighbourhood as being 'blessed with increase', and went on to say that he regarded the two years spent in the Circuit as the most useful in his life. (28) There was one particular reason why his stay in the Circuit was pleasing and that was because of the development of a close friendship with Elizabeth Crane, who he met quite early in his stay. This culminated in their marriage at St. John's in February 1787. (29) Unfortunately she only survived another seven years, dying at Halifax, where she was buried in the grounds of the Methodist Chapel.

In 1786 'Sammy' Bardsley returned to the Circuit, this time to serve as assistant to Edward Jackson with James Ridall as third man. Over the decade since he was last there the work had certainly advanced and the membership had greatly increased, so that the workload was not easy. In acknowledging this progress when writing to Bardsley, Wesley did offer a caution however, and informed him 'Brother Jackson should advise Brother Ridall not to please the devil by preaching himself to death'. (30) A typical preaching tour in the Colne Circuit for that year has fortunately been recorded, and this gives an idea of what was required of an itinerant preacher as he went about spreading the Gospel and visiting the Societies within his care. The tour covered six weeks, commencing and finishing at Colne, and during that period the preacher was planned to visit thirty nine Societies stretching from Settle in the north to Wardle Fold in the south, and from Preston in the west to Luddington (Luddenden) in the east, travelling 229 miles in the process. He was to preach on every day but two, some days twice and every Sunday three times, for a total of sixty one services. (31) It has been suggested that each of the three preachers followed a similar plan two weeks apart, but in practice it seems unlikely that this would have been strictly adhered to for all the year, nor is it certain that this pattern had been the one that had been used in earlier years. Under such a plan each preacher would see each of the others once during the six weeks, on the second and sixth Thursday of each tour when they called at Colne. Other responsibilities would interrupt the carrying out of the plan; special visits to make, an occasional conference to attend, unplanned events to deal with and sometimes illness to contend with. In addition only two horses were provided for the three preachers, so unless one of them had his own horse or was able to borrow one free of charge some of the journeys would have to be made on foot. No doubt that when necessary some of the planned services would be taken by the local preachers. Whatever planning was made had to be revised the following year when the Circuit was split into two and the Societies in the western portion and in Rossendale were grouped together to form the Blackburn Circuit.

Chapter Six

In and around Blackburn

That Blackburn should have become the head of a new Circuit would not have been thought possible less than ten years earlier, about which time there is no evidence to suggest that a Society even existed.

Amongst the earliest records of the Blackburn Circuit are the names of John and Margaret Howarth, and Rachel Houghton, who are listed in one of the membership classes in 1788, with John as the leader. (1) His class was composed of members whose places of abode were on the south side of the town in localities such as Grimshaw Park, Horse Lead, Town's Moor, Nova Scotia, Honeyhole, Darwen Street, Longshaw and even as far away as Darwen. This class appears to be the successor of what was once a separate Society known as Top o'th Coal Pits, which had started up about 1758/59 when James Oddie was a preacher in the Haworth Circuit. (2) Included in the list of members at Top o'th Coal Pits some five years into its existence were the names of John and Margaret Howarth and Rachel Houghton, together with fourteen others, amongst whom were two of John's brothers, his sister Ann Clegg and her husband James, who was the leader. (3) When the Cleggs later moved away John Howarth took his place and he continued as leader until his death in 1811. Top o'th Coal Pits, shown on early maps just on the Blackburn side of its boundary with Lower Darwen, was for a time part of the Liverpool Circuit in the 1770's, (4) until it was eventually absorbed by the new Blackburn Society within the Colne Circuit. The early membership records for Blackburn also contain the names of a few other people whose Methodist origins can be traced back to one or other of the early Societies in the vicinity, and these include George and Agnes Ainsworth. George, also a class leader at Blackburn, was described as a 'Gentleman, of Water Street', but earlier he had been a farmer at Brimmicroft where his house had been licensed for worship. (5) It was he who was, in 1759, sent as representative to the Quarterly Meeting from the Society that was then meeting at Laund and previously referred to. What part these early followers played in introducing Methodism to Blackburn proper can only be surmised, but their contribution to the new Society must surely have been creditable.

As soon as Methodism was established in the town the Society grew apace, which soon meant that it was difficult for preaching services to be held in private houses. Consequently a piece of land containing 400 square yards was obtained on lease in February 1779 by two of the members - George Walkden, a yeoman farmer, and James Tiplady, a candle maker of Darwen Street - on which piece of ground a chapel was erected. Built of brick it had two round stained glass windows facing the street, with

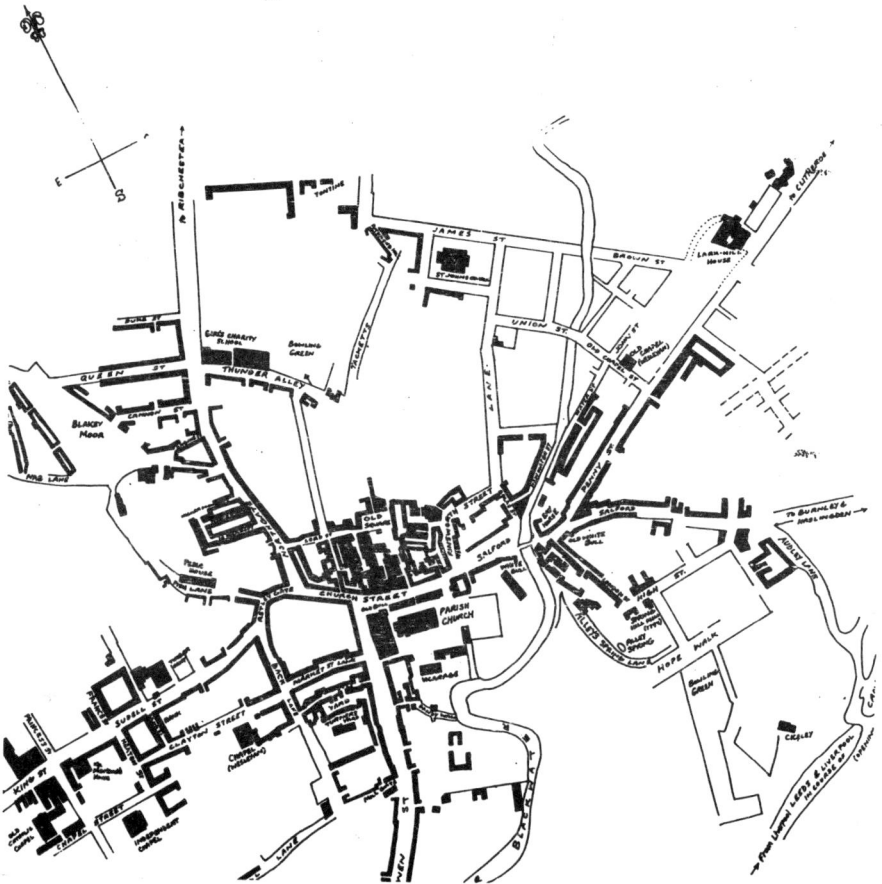

Blackburn c1795

50

a small gallery at its eastern end and adjoining the chapel a house for the preacher. (6) The site was to be found in the area of Blackburn known as Salford, on the north side of Smalley Street (later known as Old Chapel Street), which ran from Penny Street. The place is now no longer recognizable because of the creation of modern roads and developments.

Despite the building of the new chapel, there was still insufficient room to accommodate all who wished to hear John Wesley preach, when he made his first visit to Blackburn at the end of April 1780. The whole town was excited at his coming and besides those who genuinely longed to hear him there were many others who went along because of the occasion, including the leaders of the town, irrespective of whether they espoused Methodism or not. Normally with such a large crowd Wesley would have preached out of doors, but it was a hot sunny day and because of this he felt that it would be better for him to preach in the chapel. As many as could squeezed into the building, but it was unable to satisfy them all and some in the crowd were disappointed. Wesley, however, did observe that all the civic dignitaries managed to get inside to hear him, which did not entirely please him and about which he had a sharp comment to make in his Journal. (7)

Wesley visited the town in 1781, probably in 1782, and then in 1784, when he noted that the Society was lively and growing, but neither rich or well dressed. (8) By the following year the increase in the appeal of Methodism within the town caused the members to consider moving again to larger premises. With this in mind a building fund was started and George Walkden and William Banning, a baker and grocer of Astley Gate, King Street, went throughout the town obtaining gifts and promises in such a way that the amount required was almost entirely raised by these stalwarts. This was also achieved in a very short time, for on 20th December 1785 a site on Clayton Street was obtained by the Trustees and the following year a chapel was built and brought into use, at which time the old chapel, which later came to be known as Calender House because of its then use, was given up. The Clayton Street Chapel was a much larger building, set back a little from the road, with a graveyard adjoining, and was then situated in 'an open suburb, surrounded by gardens and several respectable houses of tradesmen'. (9) Whether the chapel was in use at the time Wesley came to Blackburn again in April of 1786 is not clear, because his preaching was done outdoors. The numbers in the town had been increased for it was fair-day and there was not a place large enough to contain all those who wanted to hear him. Wesley was impressed with the crowd which gathered and was able to write of the people, "All were still as night, unless when they sung; then their voices were as the sound of many waters". (10)

Since the principal aim of this book is to trace the movement of Methodism through each Circuit as it makes its advance westward to the Fylde coast, it is not possible to examine in any detail the development of all the various Societies which formed these

51

Circuits, but certainly a general look needs to be taken of the Blackburn Circuit from the records that are available. Quite a number of early records of the Clayton Street Chapel and of the Circuit have thankfully been preserved, and from them a fairly comprehensive view can be seen of the composition of the Circuit and of its growth and change during the succeeding years.

The Quarterly Meeting Cash Book and the Circuit Members Lists fully commence in 1788 and continue well into the 19th Century, but unfortunately at least one page is missing from the beginning of the Cash Book, relating to the first Quarterly Meeting which was held on 25th October 1787, undoubtedly at Blackburn, and which would have listed the names of the Societies that contributed funds to the new Circuit. It can only therefore be assumed that the names appearing in the following quarter's records are the same. Of the twenty Societies listed, fourteen of them were not known to have existed with any certainty in 1775. Besides Blackburn and Preston, eight others - Ribchester, Bolton Hall (Hoghton), Chorley, Harwood, Flaxmoss, Grane, Bank Top and Longclough - became established during the time that Colne was head of the Circuit, whilst the remaining four started up simultaneously with the new Circuit. These were Pickup Bank, Shay Houses (Whalley), Longridge and Woodplumpton - the first from the Fylde beyond Preston. (11)

Over the succeeding seven years there was a great deal of change with Societies moving both into and out of the Circuit. Some of them were transferred to other Circuits - Chorley, Wardle Fold and Longclough; several just started up and then faded away - Longton, Hoole, Lytham and Stanhill; some changed their names and locations - Grane became Bentley House and Longridge became Dutton Lee; whilst others such as Bamber Bridge, Mellor and Channel (Shorrocks Green) were formed from existing Societies. In addition new Societies were created at Accrington, Blacksnape, Facit, Upper Darwen, Rawtenstall, Poulton and Edenfield. (12)

In the past, membership records have been used to provide information about the type of person who was attracted to Methodism, because on some occasions the occupations have been quoted. Methodism's appeal had increased when the message began to be taken out to the general population and preached to people who had either not taken much of an interest in religion or attended church only out of a sense of duty. It has been suggested that it became strong in the areas where the Church of England was weak and that also much of its strength was to be found in the areas where industry was expanding, but when examined closer the membership has been found to be made up of people from every class in varying degrees. This has been borne out by work done by Dr. Clive Field in his analysis of a number of membership lists for the middle of the 18th Century, including the figures for the old Haworth Round. (13) An examination of the membership lists for the Blackburn Circuit in 1789/90 reveal that the make-up of the membership had changed but little from those Lancashire Societies included in the Haworth figures which he reviewed. The types of occupation fall mainly into four categories and are shown below as a percentage of 380 male members whose occupations are listed. Figures for 1763/4 covering 195 members are shown for comparison. (14)

	1789/90	1763/4
Farmers	3.9	12.3
Merchants & Tradesmen	18.7	12.8
Manufacturers	70.0	71.3
Labourers, Miners and other miscellaneous manual workers	5.3	3.1
Other	2.1	0.5
	100.0	100.0

As will be obvious to those who know anything about this area of Lancashire in the 18th Century, 'cotton was king', and it gave employment to many thousands of people, mainly in their own homes. Whilst the spinning of cotton soon became a factory based industry following the mechanical inventions this mainly affected the women, but the same could not be said for weaving which was done by the men and which remained largely unchanged until well into the 19th Century. Up to the sudden fall in prices in the 1820's weavers were relatively well off and independent. It was common for them to own their own loom and possibly their cottage and because of this distinctive form of employment they were able to preserve an independent way of life which sometimes surprised their social superiors. (15) The high percentage shown in the table for 'Manufacturers' reflects the considerable number involved in this cottage based industry, where in 1789/90 there were 220 men identified as 'cotton weavers' out of a total of 261 who could be classified as being in the textile trade. From the figures quoted it can thus be seen that most of the members were gathered from amongst a group who had a certain amount of independency and were not directly subject to a master or overlord.

On the other hand it has been pointed out that the names of the members appearing on the lists only belong to people who had made a commitment to Methodism, but there were also others, not recorded, who were less skilled belonging to the labouring classes who had an affinity with Methodism, who should not be overlooked when estimating the strength and make-up of the movement. It has been estimated that at the time of John Wesley's death there were three times as many adherants as there were members.

It should not be assumed, however, that most in this group came from the less skilled section of society. Indeed there was an ever increasing number who came from the more independent class. (16) The commitment which the members of a Methodist Society had to make in pursuit of their beliefs required a good deal of courage and discipline, for it was not just a matter of attending worship services. The Class Meeting was at the centre of the Society, with weekly attendance expected. Here in fellowship with like-minded people, through devotion and prayer, through testimony, discussion and confession of sins, the members renewed each others faith so that they were better able to reflect their beliefs in their everyday lives. The commitment also involved a financial obligation, often given sacrificially, towards the work of the Society and the support of the preachers in the Circuit. Sometimes this onus of membership proved too much over a prolonged period for a percentage of people and caused them to give up their commitment, whilst still retaining some allegiance to the cause. It is difficult to determine how many of those giving up their membership, because of the discipline of commitment, completely turned away from Methodism, but it seems reasonable to assume that many of them would still retain some interest.

An analysis of the membership lists for Blackburn Circuit for the four years from 1788 to 1792 for eight of the Societies shows that the turnover was fairly high. Based on average figures for each year 106 members were lost from a total of 485 whilst 136 members were being added. Using these figures a complete turnover of membership would occur every four and a half years. Lists for the years 1796/97 were also compared covering fifteen Societies in the Circuit which shows that out of 839 members, 158 were lost whilst 172 new ones were added for a turnover of 5.3 years. If a similar pattern was followed until the end of the century consider the number of lives which Methodism had influenced - almost three times the actual membership, and this does not account for those others who never actually became members.

It has been shown that the growth of the Blackburn Society was fairly rapid but even this does not compare with the growth of the Society at Upper Darwen. About 1788 a young man called William Greenwood from Darwen was on his way to Preston Races when he was stopped and spoken to by William Banning. The latter expressed his concern about a tragic accident which had occurred at these races on the previous day, and by the conversation was able to dissuade young Greenwood from his pursuit. Not only that, he was persuaded to change his way of life and was soon to be found attending the Methodist Chapel in Blackburn, where he began subscribing for a seat in the gallery. Shortly after this he became the instigator of the cause of Darwen, where a room over a blacksmith's shop in Wellington Fold became the meeting place. Within weeks William and two of his friends, Richard Cross and William Crook, had taken over another room on Water Street, above an alleyway which led to Peggy Brook. At first the group only contained the three of them and four others, and it was run as a class under the Blackburn Society, but a year later the number had doubled and it became a separate Society, with Greenwood as leader. By 1791 there were forty four members and in need of larger premises, so a plot of land was obtained at Back Lane, and a chapel built and opened within a very short time that year. By the following July the membership had doubled yet again, this time to ninety, to become the fourth largest in the Circuit - larger even than Preston. William Greenwood and his two friends are reported to have come from Poulton Parish to establish themselves in their respective

Facsimile pages from the Blackburn Circuit Membership Lists.
(Courtesy of the Circuit Archivist, Wesley Hall, Blackburn)

trades in Darwen, but they did more than that and all within four years and because a young man gave up his pleasure of a day at the races. (17)

At Preston the room which the Society had been using in St. John Street began to get overcrowded, so a decision was made to build a chapel and soon a site was found on the west side of Back Lane. Largely through the generosity of Roger Crane and his father a chapel was erected in 1787. (18) The building can be clearly identified on Shakeshaft's 1809 map of Preston at the junction of Plant's Court (Lowthian Street), showing the preachers house adjoining it to the south, with a piece of ground fronting them both along Back Lane. Opposite lay open land stretching for some distance. It is reported that to get to the chapel Martha Whitehead used to walk across Chadwick Orchard from her home in Turks Head Court. Back Lane could also be approached from the Market Place northwards along Anchor Wiend, from whence the lane roughly followed the line of an arc, passing through Starch House Square, on the east side of and practically the whole length of Friargate - undoubtedly following the boundary line of the medieval tofts on that side of this principal street.

In 1790 when Wesley made his last visit to Preston he preached on three occasions, but there is no indication in his diary as to whether any of it was done in the chapel, although there is a very strong tradition that he preached both in the Market Place and the chapel (19) One extraordinary event that did take place there was when Nanny Cutler and Mary Barritt visited the chapel by invitation in 1794 and conducted the service. They were the means by which some were converted, including a young man called Lawrence Disley, who had walked from Salwick after work especially to hear them, and who in his turn would have an influence on the lives of others as a Class Leader at Poulton. Mary Barritt was one of the most successful evangelists among the first Methodist women preachers and by the consistent results of her preaching she was able to overcome the determined opposition that had been aroused by her methods. (20) Indeed, right from the age of nineteen as a member of the Colne Society, she had done some exhorting in the vicinity of her home at Foulridge, but was reprimanded by Lancelot Harrison (1792/4), the preacher at Colne, for so doing. Credit must be given him though for changing his mind when he could see the success she had in winning people over. (21)

The Preston membership at this time was fairly static, with numbers hovering around eighty, but the turnover of members was higher than the Circuit average, with some of the original stalwarts such as Isabel Walmsley, her son William, and Martha Whitehead missing from the later returns. To compensate for this new names began to appear of people who were destined to support and give life to the Society in the years ahead - e.g. Parker, Cooper, Holden, Smith and Singleton. The Society was divided into five classes under the leadership of :-
Michael Emmet - (until he moved to Blackburn), followed by Thos. Holden.

Thomas Crane - a Local Preacher, son of Samuel and cousin of Roger, who had an ironmongery business in Market Place.

John Hoskinson, followed by John Leece - a Local Preacher and whitesmith of Wood Street.

John Walmsley - another Local Preacher and Steward to Sir Henry de Hoghton, who lived at Cooper Hill, Walton le Dale, in which place the Class Meetings were held.

Roger Crane - still very much involved.

In September 1791 the Walton le Dale Class changed its name to Bamber Bridge and became a separate Society which (for a time at least) encompassed Clayton le Woods. (22) This was probably following the sudden death of John Walmsley. The principal of the cause in the area now became George Hilton, who together with his wife Mary and four children had been members since 1788/89. George's father had died in 1748 when he was only seven years old and because of difficulties which arose as a result of his mother's subsequent marriage he did not receive his inheritance until 1771. Included in this was forty acres of land and the Old Hall, which was described as being adjacent to the bridge known as Bamber Bridge, and it was here that the Hilton family lived. In January 1793 this became the meeting place for the local Society and remained so for another twenty eight years until a chapel was built. (23)

Reference has already been made to the Societies of Hoole and Longton, which faded after a while. There does not seem to be any known reference to the meeting place at Hoole, but at Longton it is known that the house of John Baxendale was registered for worship in January 1788, but no denomination is indicated in the record. (24) Methodism had been introduced into the village whilst William Bramwell was still at Preston and he was responsible for the conversion of John Parke, who was involved in the subsequent work there, so there is every likelihood that for a time there was a meeting place in the area. The Society does appear in the Circuit Book for two quarters at the beginning of 1790 as contributing funds, so membership classes must have been held prior to this. (25)

The Fylde folk were also slow in establishing Methodism in their midst. They were conservative and traditional in their ways and practically all of them followed the faith of their fathers, be it Anglican or Roman Catholic. The only outstanding representative of organized nonconformity up to the latter part of the Eighteenth Century was the Independent Chapel at Elswick, which had been started in the second half of the previous century. Judging from the baptismal records, it attracted a few from a wider area, in addition to the villages in close proximity; these include folk from Stalmine, Poulton, Carleton, Thornton, Bispham with Norbreck, Layton with Warbreck and Marton. For a time the latter place had received visits from some of Ingham's preachers, and in 1762 the house of Robert Fisher was established as a meeting place for that cause, but after a short while the support from the preachers faded away and the members eventually united themselves with Elswick. (26) The Quakers too had some small bands of followers in places such as Out Rawcliffe, Poulton, Eccleston, Freckleton and Woodplumpton, but by the end of the century they had declined in strength.

One further place where nonconformity had found a foothold, but then faded, was at Bispham where there seems to have been some vestige of a meeting place for the Presbyterians in the vicinity of the old Endowed School. Although never strong there is evidence that some of the families living in and around Bispham had been influenced by this independent spirit. It is significant that from out of such families, amongst whom were the Bambers and Roskells of Great Bispham, the Daggers of Graddle Slack Farm, and the Hodgsons of Warbreck Rakes, came some who were later responsible for promoting and supporting both Methodism and Congregationalism in the area.

As indicated above, forming part of the Blackburn Circuit by the end of 1787 was a small Society at Woodplumpton, with a membership of fourteen under the leadership of Thomas Clarkson. Considering that Methodism had by then been in existence nationally for fifty years it was not an earth-shattering event. Nevertheless it does seem worthwhile to recall the names of the members, for it is of some significance, being the first official record of Methodists in the Fylde outside of Preston. (27) They were Thomas Clarkson (shoemaker), Nancy Wood, Thomas Hardman (weaver of Salwick), Elizabeth Westcoat, Thomas Hodgkinson (farmer of Eccleston), Mary Fairclough (spinster), John Watson (joiner of Plumpton), Nancy Watson, Ellen Watson (spinster), Robert Ward, Peggy Hyde (spinster), Mary Ward, Mary Copeland (spinster of Plumpton Hall) and Alice Threlfall (spinster). It is not known where the first meeting place was located, but by the beginning of 1793 the Society was established at the home of John and Nancy Watson, (28) who were to devote their lives in serving the cause in the vicinity until well into the 1820's. In 1812 John conveyed land and buildings to fifteen Methodist Trustees, whose intention was to eventually build a chapel on the site. (29) Although there were also others in the village and surrounding area who supported Methodism, for some reason, between the commencement of the original Society and the purchase of the Watson land, there was an interruption to the meetings at Woodplumpton and the Society either ceased for a time, or what is more likely, moved to some nearby parish or township; possibly Broughton, which appears on the 1809 Preston Circuit plan. (30)

Some of the visits which the Local Preachers from Preston had made into other parts of the Fylde now began to bear fruit. The message that was preached became more effective as more preaching places were opened at Churchtown, Poulton, Thornton and Lytham. At the latter place James Lyons, who was in the Circuit for a few months, (31) was able to persuade James Marcer to open up his cottage in Fisherman's Row (Bath Street) at the end of 1792 and establish a Society, which lasted about a year before it declined. (32) Despite this the Marcer family retained their new found faith and preserved the house as a meeting place for the occasional preacher who came along.

James was later to write a number of hymns and have them published through the generosity of a friend under the title of 'The Fisherman's Hymns'. (33) At Churchtown Roger Crane with two of his Preston friends, John Leece and John Cooper, had promoted the opening of the house of Richard Dickinson in 1791 for use as a place of worship, (34) but again it does not seem as if anything permanent was set up until the turn of the century at which time it was administered from the Lancaster Circuit. Richard Dickinson stayed faithful and his name appears again in later records for his village.

At Poulton things were more successful where meetings began in 1792, since which time there has been nothing to suggest that the Society has not been continuous right up to the present time. The earliest preaching place seems to have been at the house of Edmund Singleton, (35) a merchant of the town and a member of a well established local family, but it did not survive owing to his untimely death the following spring. Soon however, a new place was found at premises on Ball Street in the shadow of St. Chad's Church and near to its north west gate. This was at the home of Robert Harrison, a wheelwright, who had also given encouragement a little earlier to his kinsman Thomas Harrison, when the latter's home at Limebreast, Thornton was opened to a group of Methodists. (36)

During the time that many of these events were taking place within the Blackburn Circuit there was a great deal that was affecting Methodism nationally.

Following the death of John Wesley the hopes, still held by a few, that Methodism could function as an evangelical body within the Church of England, were quickly dashed. The practical difficulties regarding preaching times, ordination and the sacraments, as well as other problems, which Wesley had managed to control for most of the time, soon were being debated by the varying shades of opinion within the movement. It became not a question of whether to separate from the Church but as to what direction to take. Various problems came to the fore - the question of who should administer the Holy Communion; the powers of Trustees and of Conference; the authority of the Class Leaders: and the position of Wesley's preachers and lay preachers. There were many shades of opinion and a lot was said and done until in 1795 a compromise was decided upon which was accepted by most and which eventually led to the formation of the Methodist Church.

The few who did not accept the compromise were very active and vociferous and were led by a preacher who, like Wesley, had been born at Epworth. He was Alexander Kilham and those who followed him became known at Kilhamities. Such was the manner of his opposition that it resulted in his expulsion by the Methodist Conference in the following year, and having attracted six other preachers to him they founded the Methodist New Connexion, the first of the major breakaways that was to plague Methodism over the following fifty years or so. (37)

Chapter Seven

A Detour via Wigan

After the Conference of 1794 there was a re-alignment of Circuits in Lancashire, and Blackburn lost the Societies of Preston, Plumpton, Bamber Bridge, Poulton and Hoole, which became part of the Wigan Circuit that had been created the previous year. (1) There are no extant Circuit records to show that this was the case, but evidence can be found in two baptismal registers to confirm the fact.

The separation of Methodism from the Established Church meant that the baptisms of Methodist children need no longer be conducted and recorded in the local parish church. Such ceremonies began to be carried out by the Methodist preachers, and separate records were maintained. Whilst such events usually took place in the meeting rooms or chapels of the local Societies by one of the Circuit preachers or his representative, the entries were often, though not always, recorded centrally for the whole of the Circuit at the principal chapel in a Circuit register. Unfortunately the care of maintaining and preserving some of these early records was not as it should have been, resulting in the loss of quite a few registers, including that for Wigan Circuit.

There was, however, a separate register kept for the baptisms which were held at Lamberhead Green, Pemberton from 1796 which is still extant, showing that the officiating ministers were Thomas Wood (1796-7), Thomas Hutton (1797-8) and John Furness (1798-9). These names can be confirmed as preachers in the Wigan Circuit from other sources. A comparison of the names of these ministers with those in a Preston Baptismal register shows that for the years shown the names are identical, which can only lead one to assume that those preachers appointed to the Wigan Circuit were also responsible for Preston. Although the Preston register does not properly commence until 1798, there is a statement on the first page referring to an earlier register, possibly the missing Wigan one, from which a few entries have been transcribed into the new register. These relate to the children of Thomas and Betty Cornwell (Cornall) of Woodplumpton and other children of Preston families. The officiating ministers were the three already identified. (2) Coming at a time when, nationally, Methodism was trying to resolve the way it was to go, the move to the Wigan Circuit could not have been helpful for the Societies formerly connected with Blackburn and especially so for those beyond Preston. They found themselves considerably further away from the centre of administration and the hub of things and in addition, in 1795, the complement of ministers in the new Circuit was reduced from three to two. (3) The paucity of records does not assist in understanding how things were and it is difficult to know if a man such as Roger Crane who had done so much work in serving as Circuit Steward for Blackburn, was as highly regarded or had the same influence in the new set up.

Another disturbing factor was that the Kilhamite controversy came to the fore in Lancashire, especially in Bolton and Wigan, but it was also felt in Blackburn and Preston. Two letters are particularly enlightening regarding how the dispute affected the area, and developments could have been much different if some had not had second thoughts. By 1790 Michael Emmet and his wife had moved their home from Preston to Blackburn, where they lived at Chapel Green adjoining the Clayton Street Chapel, and where they entertained Wesley in April that year. (4) Following the move, Michael remained at Blackburn only just over a year before becoming a Methodist preacher at Alnwick, at the same time as a Henry Taylor was moved to serve at Blackburn. Whether the two men met or knew each other at this time is uncertain, but at least Emmet would have an interest in the work Taylor was doing amongst his friends. Over the next few years however, they did develop similar thoughts over the problems that were besetting Methodism, so much so that for a time they sided with Alexander Kilham, but they did not follow him into the New Connexion, although Taylor did tender his resignation to Conference, but then withdrew it. A letter written in August 1797 from Bolton by Benjamin Hunt to Kilham, the day after their first Conference had ended, stated "We are informed here that Messrs. Taylor and Emmet have left you and gone over to Conference again; if so, we believe, you are better without the men that are not steady ....." (5) Although Emmet was no longer living in his home town it must be remembered that he still had family connections in Preston. His brother Richard, and wife Catherine, together with other Emmets were connected with the Back Lane chapel, and also his own wife was Roger Crane's sister, so it is possible that some of them, as well as his friends, were influenced by his leanings to the new faction. The second letter gives some credence along these lines. This was sent by John Wood to Kilham in October 1797 informing him "......we shall try to get into Blackburn.....There has been some letters passing between Preston and Sheffield and that you have lost all your friends at P. Mr. C. will not take you into his house any more...." (6) It seems that there is every possibility that the Mr. C. referred to was Roger Crane, and if so Kilham must have been a guest at his home at an earlier date, when he was one of his supporters. The preacher is known to have come to Preston, by invitation from some of the members, in either December 1796 or January 1797 and is reported to have been respectfully received. (7)

An intriguing connection involving Emmet, Kilham and members of the Crane family was the town of Alnwick, Northumberland. Emmet's appointment there has already been referred to, but his brother in law, who had married Roger Crane's other sister was there 1791-93, whilst Kilham was appointed to that place in 1795 when the controversy was raging. As for Roger, his connection was through his first wife, the former Mary Annett of High House, Alnwick, who he had married at the beginning of that year but who he had been visiting since 1792. (8) During the summer of 1796 Mary spent several weeks in Blackpool because of her ill health, but unfortunately died later in that year, giving Roger less reasons to visit the Northumbrian town. Since Alnwick was fairly prompt in establishing a New Connexion Society the possibility that the religious and social climate of the town had an influence on those who had interests there has to be considered.

From the comments that were made in the letters quoted above it seems that for a while the danger of the New Connexion establishing itself in Preston and Blackburn had passed, but the same could not be said for Wigan. Here the members oscillated over the support which they gave to the breakaway movement, and on more than one occasion the loyal members were forced to vacate the chapel and rent a room in which to hold their meetings. By early January 1798 the New Connexion membership had reached thirty two and at nearby Goose Green there were ten; Blackrod had eighteen, whilst Bolton had grown to 135. (9) Irrespective of any direct influence in the Society, the disruption at Wigan must have had repercussions throughout the Circuit, especially seeing that it was the base from which the travelling preacher worked. Administration would be all the more difficult and the forced move from the chapel premises undoubtedly contributed to the loss of some of the records. The Conference of 1799 recognized the difficulties that were being encountered and reversed the roles of the Wigan and Preston Societies, making the latter head of the Circuit, whilst waiting thirteen more years before permanently re-establishing Wigan in such a way.

The task of trying to determine the composition of the Preston Circuit is just as difficult as it was for its predecessor, since the surviving records are just as meagre. Apart from the baptismal register, information has to be gleaned mainly from secondary sources, and here there is but little available that has not been referred to in earlier histories of Preston Methodism. Up to 1809 when a Circuit plan can be made use of, the names of the Societies have to be deduced. The number could not have been large at the end of the first year, since there were only 373 members in the whole Circuit. Based on what is known of the area and past developments it would appear as if the following places would be contained in it - Preston, Wigan, Lamberhead Green, Chorley, Bamber Bridge, Dutton Lee (or Longridge), Woodplumpton (or a nearby community) and Poulton. Probably by this time there was also a Society at Longton, and possibly at Garstang and Brinscal. During the five years before Preston was made into a Circuit people were using meeting houses at Windy Harbour, near Wheelton, Ribby with Wrea, and possibly at Moon's Mill (Upper Walton), but there is no evidence to suggest that they had developed into Societies by 1799. (10) One further difficulty in determining the Circuit's composition in this embryonic period is the uncertainty of its boundaries, which often seemed to be changing. Wigan, and presumably others in that area, flitted in and out of the Circuit twice before finally leaving in 1803, and this in its turn also caused the total membership to fluctuate. Between 1801-02 numbers fell to 275.

Besides Wigan dropping out of the Circuit that year, there was an additional reason for the fall in membership in 1801 - the New Connexion. Having seemingly escaped this problem a few years previous, several in the Preston Society now espoused this cause and there was strife within the fellowship. A group of sympathizers managed to obtain the keys to the Back Lane chapel and almost prevented the faithful members from entering, but fortunately it was not successful. (11) The strife, however, continued until a number left to form a New Connexion Society. By October 1803 they had managed to acquire a warehouse on Lord Street, belonging to a William Summerfield, and have it registered for worship, staying there until 1816. The petition for this registration reveals some of the names of those who supported this new venture. They were Samuel Parker, Thomas Emmet (brother of Michael), Thomas Holden, William Summerfield, Miles Leo, John Hodgkinson and Clayton Aspden. (12) The names of other supporters who officiated at baptisms were Mr. Myers, John Drake, John Talbot, John Wood, John Hickson, William Walmsley and George Smith, some of whom would be local men. (13) The loss of members from Back Lane affected the life and witness of the Society. From the few names mentioned it can be seen that family loyalties were divided and former leaders were lost. By the summer of 1804 the Circuit membership had sunk to 255 and at Conference only one preacher was appointed as a result. Apparently not all the followers stayed on in the new group and some gradually drifted back. Amongst these was Clayton Aspden, for by 1809 he was back on the Circuit plan of the parent body and in 1812 was supporting the original cause at Leyland. (14)

Because the New Connexion Societies were formed as a result of splinter groups breaking away from the parent body over Methodist policy they were to be found in places where Methodism had been firmly established, like Wigan, Bolton, Preston and Blackburn (where by 1800 there were 48 members). In other areas, especially to the west beyond Preston, the new body did not seem to have any impact and it was to be almost ninety years before such a Society was formed in Blackpool. Gradually the Back Lane Society recovered from the disruption to its witness and soon some of its members and local preachers were helping to introduce their brand of Methodism into some of the neighbouring communities. Even during the turmoil and shortly following, attempts at establishing Methodism were made again at Lytham, followed by Leyland and Head Nook, Myerscough. (15) None of these, however, appear on the 1809 Preston Circuit plan. (16) This peculiar system which the Methodists adopted had developed over the years and began to be printed on a regular basis to indicate the preachers appointed to take services at the various Societies within the Circuit, over a period of three months or sometimes longer. It is a useful source of information, for not only does the plan list the preaching places but it gives the times and frequency of the services and lists all the preachers, both travelling and local. In 1809 at Preston there were two and ten preachers respectively. The one thing that it does not distinguish is whether or not the preaching place was a chapel or a cottage, etc. This plan shows that at Preston,

Chorley, Brinscal, Longton, (all of which had chapels by then) and Moon's Mill services were held every Sunday, with all except the latter having more than one service. At Bamber Bridge, Clayton le Woods, Broughton, Goosnargh and Longridge there were fortnightly services, whilst at Poulton two services were held on one Sunday each month. These were the only places where services were planned.

When compared with the distances that the early Methodist preachers had to travel in the Haworth and Colne Circuits, together with the larger number of members that they were responsible for, it would seem that the travelling preachers at the turn of the century were not hard pressed. With the support that was being given by the local preachers it surely could have been possible for them to have got about the Circuit more. The Preston plan shows that between April and October, at a period of the year when travelling would have been easier, neither of the travelling preachers deemed it worth their while to preach a Sunday service at Longton, Bamber Bridge, Clayton, Goosnargh, Longridge or Poulton. The practice of generally excluding local preachers from the central pulpits obviously worked against Societies further afield. Had the preachers lost their missionary zeal, or was it a case of those who supported them and the Circuit most financially demanding their services? Why was it that no new permanent Society had been set up in the Fylde beyond the immediate area about Preston since 1793, despite some interest being shown? It is inconceivable to think that the Fylde folk were that conservative. The situation, however, was gradually being addressed, and although the Preston Circuit would eventually share in the work the ancient Hundred of Amounderness was already receiving attention from another direction.

In order to look at the direction from whence this came it is first necessary to look again at the Blackburn Circuit records, which reveal that in June 1788, included in the grand total of members for the Circuit, there were eleven from a Society meeting at Lancaster; although they did not contribute to Circuit funds. This was the only occasion that they were included in the reported total, for they soon were under the care of the Colne preachers. A note of 3rd July 1790 in the Blackburn Circuit book makes reference to this. Methodism in the region about Lancaster began to expand fairly quickly and by 1794 the city was established as the head of a new Circuit, with Abraham Moseley as preacher in charge. The following year a chapel was opened at the corner of Wood Street and Damside Street. Most of the Societies in the Circuit were to be found north of the city, but for a time there was one at Garstang, with six members included in it. This did not seem to last for after 1796 these members were shown as being 'removed', but there is no clear indication as to whether this was because they had ceased to meet or because they had become the responsibility of another Circuit. Whatever the reason this time, it seems certain that Garstang must have been in the Preston Circuit a few years later, for after the realignment of the Lancaster Circuit in 1804, when it gave up a number of Societies to the Kendal Circuit, Garstang reverted

A SABBATH-DAY'S PLAN,

FOR THE TRAVELLING AND LOCAL PREACHERS,

In the Preston Circuit, from April 16, to October 22, 1809.

Names:

1. —. Lumb.
2. J. Johnson.
3. R. C.
4. J. Leece.
5. E. Leece.
6. T. Shorrock.
7. C. Aspden.
8. W. Cooper.
9. J. Gregory.
10. J. Butterfield
11. R. Yates.
12. R. Allen.

Places & Times, 1809.	April	May	June	July	August	Sep.	October
Preston 10¼ & 6.							
Chorley 10¾ & 2.							
Ditto........6.							
Brinscal 10¾ & 2.							
Longton, 2¼ & 6.							
Moon's-Mill..3.							
Bamber-Bridge 6.							
Clayton......2.							
Broughton....2.							
Goosnargh...2.							
Longridge....2.							
Poulton..2 & 6.							

N. B. S. Sacrament. L. Lovefeast. Quarter-days, June 22, and Sep. 21.

to Lancaster and a few months later was reporting twenty eight members. (17) Soon Stoops Hall, which was tenanted by one of the members, Thomas Coughtry, began to be used as the Society's meeting place and services were held there. (18) The two preachers based in Lancaster Circuit were now able to give much more attention to the rural areas about Garstang and there is evidence of Methodists living in Catterall, Scorton and the area about Wyresdale. (19) Being a market town, news of the increased presence of the preachers was quick to reach other areas in Amounderness and by 1806 an invitation had been given for one of them to visit Preesall, in Stalmine Parish. From the resulting visit the house of Thomas Ronson was set apart for the use of future preachers, and it became the forerunner of other meeting places in the vicinity. (20) (Over thirty years later other members of the Ronson family would open up their home to the infant Society at Fleetwood).

Together with renewed efforts from the direction of Preston, these new ventures into Amounderness gradually began to have an influence on the state of Methodism there.

Living in Preston at this time was a young man who was destined to make a name for himself in the field of astronomy, both as an inventor and lecturer, and his achievements were later so recognized that he was made a Freeman of the town in 1834. His name was Moses Holden who was born at Bolton in 1777, son of Thomas and Joyce. (21) The family moved to Preston where, by 1789, his parents had joined the Back Lane Society, and after a further year Thomas had become a Class Leader. When Moses was about eighteen he was influenced by Roger Crane and he joined the Methodist Society and eventually became a local preacher. This was some time shortly after the summer of 1809, for he does not appear on the Circuit plan for that period. He was later to become an active member of the Preston Temperance movement and a friend of Joseph Livesey.

In January 1811 he was persuaded by Thomas Jackson, the preacher stationed at Preston, to spend some time preaching to the people who desired to hear about Methodism in Amounderness. During the first six months of that year he visited different parts of the area and thankfully he recorded details of some of his experiences in his Journal, extracts from which in 1885 were in the possession of William Henry Hincksman of Lytham, who like his father before him was a great influence in the development of the Methodist churches in the Blackpool and Lytham areas. (22) Moses commenced his evangelistic work on 19th January by travelling to Poulton, where he arrived in the evening. He chose this place as his starting point for it was "...the only place where Methodism had made any way, and here there were ten members". He states that he was entertained at the home of John and Betty Tomlinson, from where John drove him to the various nearby villages. The day after he arrived was a Sunday and he preached twice at Thornton, also at Poulton, and then the day after at Little Marton. On another occasion when visiting Bispham he was opposed by the incumbent

Rev. William Elston, a dour parson who had been born at Mythop of the well known local family, and who served Bispham for forty years. The entry in Holden's Journal records "One day when I had to preach there some of the people begged I would not go...for Mr. Elston said he would have me put in prison. I said that would be an honour. I went and preached without any disturbance." Another Sunday James Morrow, the Congregational minister of Poulton, sent word that he had better not go to Bispham for "...he was well assured that the clergyman had engaged several men to kill me, and they were to have ale and rum mixed, to fit them for their work. Many came to persuade me not to go....for the clergyman had threatened.......everyone who either lent me a chair or allowed me to stand on their horse block". As it was he was driven there in a shandry and he used it for a pulpit. True to the warning during the preaching service a number of men appeared and some of the congregation were alarmed, but the preacher simply invited them to come closer and listen to what he had to say. Then he told the crowd not to worry about any disturbance since they would be protected by the law of the land and by God. Hearing this, the would be trouble makers were stopped in their tracks and they stood where they were throughout the service, which finished in peace.

By the time summer came his responsibility for the area was over, for at the Conference that year most of Amounderness was placed in a new Circuit centred on Garstang. He recorded in his Journal the then existing Societies, together with their membership, and although the numbers seem exceedingly small Methodism had established itself in a few more places. As has already been pointed out elsewhere the influence of Methodism would have affected a far greater number of people than the numbers of members would suggest. What seems to have been lacking in some of the places was a local person strong enough to hold a group together during the times when the travelling preachers were not directly amongst them. The Societies listed in the Journal were - Poulton-11, Rawcliffe-2, St. Michaels-7, Kirkham-8, Marton-7, Thornton-17, Freckleton-12, and Preesall-16. He was unable to persuade those who were interested at Lytham to form themselves into a Society, and likewise he was unsuccessful at Bispham. About Lytham he wrote, "They received me kindly, and heard me gladly, but that was all". Undoubtedly the attitude of the incumbents at Lytham and Bispham had much to do with it.

Chapter Eight

Pioneers in the Fylde

The statement which Holden made about Poulton being the only place where Methodism had made any headway seems in need of an explanation, when it can be seen that, from the Societies he listed, there were others with similar or larger membership. Poulton Society, however, had much more of a history than the others, stretching back for about eighteen years, whereas Freckleton was only begun about the summer of 1810, following an earlier visit of Holden, and Preesall was but five years old. Thornton's origins go as far back as those of Poulton, but there is no reference to it in the Blackburn Circuit records and neither is there anything which suggests that meetings continued for any length of time, until it was re-established at the beginning of 1809.

The continuance of the Poulton Society throughout its early period is largely attributable to members of the Gaskell family, which produced men and women who were strong enough to support and keep together those who were desirous of following the way of Methodism and they were also the inspiration of other Methodists who were starting up locally. The Methodists in Poulton, as has been shown, were meeting at the house of Robert Harrison from January 1794 and two of those who were petitioners for its registration were John and Joseph Gaskell. (1) A closer look at this family is called for.

The Gaskells were settled in the Norbeck area of Bispham Parish by the beginning of the 17th Century and were to remain there for 130 years, whilst other branches could be found close by at Thornton and Bispham well into more modern times. Sometime about 1670, one of the Norbreck line - John - moved with his family across the River Wyre to Hambleton and settled at Bank House, and from this branch the Methodist family has descended. (2) John and Isabelle Gaskell were having children there during the 1740's and 1750's, amongst whom were the John and Joseph mentioned above, as well as Thomas, Ellen and Margaret. Isabelle was the daughter of Thomas Hodskinson, whose younger namesake was one whose name appears on the 1788 list of members at Woodplumpton. It was about this time that both John and Isabelle died, so it is not known if they were ever influenced by Methodism, but since all of their children supported the cause it seems likely that there must have been some principal source of influence. Joseph, the youngest of the three brothers, had moved to Poulton by the 1780's where he ran a woollen drapery business and where he came into contact with Edmund Singleton, the merchant who was later to establish the first Methodist meeting place in the town. These two men, with others, were also party to a deed in 1785 relating

Terrace on the south side of Ball Street, Poulton,
- site of an early Methodist Meeting House.

to a property near Anchorsholme, which later came to be known as Bispham Court. (3) Perhaps as a result of the common business bond between them there may also have arisen some mutual attraction to Methodism. Besides joining with his brother John in the petitioning of the Harrison meeting house, they were also petitioners for a house at Ribby with Wray in 1795 belonging to their married sister Margaret Nickson. (4) Joseph, however, was in a poor state of health and by the summer of 1798 he had given up his business in Poulton and before two years was up he had died and was buried at Hambleton. His property at Out Rawcliffe and most of his estate was distributed amongst his brothers and sisters.

The eldest brother John inherited the farm at Bank after his father's death and he remained there for many years, but eventually he also became a woollen draper in Poulton and it was through him that the Poulton Society found a more permanent home in which to meet in 1799.

The market place in Poulton today, as it has done for many a year, welcomes many visitors and sightseers who are attracted to the town because it has been able to retain some of its originality and reminders of the past, set against the background of the old parish church. Spacious as the market square may seem at present it was even more so 250 years ago, when it extended further to the west following the line down from the west side of Church Street. After a fire which occurred in 1732 to the low thatched buildings on that side of the market place a new row of houses was eventually erected in front of the old building line, leaving the former row to develop into an array of miscellaneous buildings. (5) It was to here that the Society moved and it became their home for the next twenty years. This place of worship was described in the registration petition as "a certain Building belonging to John Gaskell of Poulton - gent - situate and being on the west side or back part of the north end of a certain Row of houses called the new Buildings which form the west side of the Market Place in Poulton". (6) The site is behind where the Royal Bank of Scotland now stands.

Based on records that are available, Thomas, who lived at 'Brickhouse' in Staynall, does not seem to have been as involved in the work as his brothers were during the period of their lifetime, but shortly after John's death in 1808 Thomas was supporting James Parkinson, a clockmaker of Stalmine, whose house was dedicated for worship. (7) He also becomes more involved at a later date. His sister Margaret Nickson has been mentioned, but she also had a widowed daughter, Bella, who supported her at the starting up of the Ribby fellowship. The latter married again in 1798, this time to George Thompson of Out Rawcliffe, where he had a small farm, but they soon had removed to Preston and he became a cheesemonger. Supporting Methodism as they did they were quickly connected with the Back Lane Chapel, where, according to the register, four of their children were baptized. (8) Their marriage, which had taken place at St. Michaels Parish Church, was one half of a double ceremony, with the other parties being her cousin Mary Dagger and William Whitehead, and to which ceremonies Bella's brother Robert was witness. Just as the Thompson children were baptized at the Back Lane Chapel, so also were some of the children of William and Mary Whitehead, with one of the baptismal entries being of especial note. This is the entry on 19th March 1803 which records the baptism of Ellen Whitehead, daughter of William and Mary of Mountains, near Poulton - the first from the western part of the Fylde. Earlier than this two of their children had been baptized at Elswick Congregational Church.

William seems to have been born in this village in 1772, about the time that William Bramwell was leaving to serve his apprenticeship at Preston, and he grew up to become a weaver there. During the early years of the marriage their home was in Elswick and then Thistleton. The designation of 'Mountains' is somewhat of a mystery as the early maps do not give any clue to its whereabouts, but which ought not to be too difficult to locate amongst the flatter lands of the area. Nevertheless the puzzle remains. It could have been in the Thistleton area where the Whiteheads were in 1800, but if so, to describe it as being 'near Poulton' is most unusual. 'Mountains' can be identified as a field name on the 1848 Tithe map of Bispham, and part of its boundary is still recognizable today on the North Shore golf links. It lies just to the south of Graddle Slack farm where Mary's parents, Thomas and Ellen Dagger, had once lived, but as they moved to the Skippool area of Thornton around 1784 and since there is no evidence of a homestead in the large field, to associate it with the Whiteheads seems somewhat tenuous. A third possibility is in the Thornton area where the family had settled near to the rest of the Dagger family, by 1810.

Thomas Dagger, who had married Ellen Gaskell about 1772, came from a long line of Bispham Daggers, which extended back into the Elizabethan period. Both Thomas's and Ellen's predecessors must have been near neighbours in earlier times. On giving up Graddle Slack farm Thomas sold it to none other than Edmund Singleton, and he was also another of the parties to the deed relating to the Anchorsholme property. After they had moved to Thornton the last two of the five girls who survived to adulthood were born, shortly before the death of their father in 1791. Despite this loss, the family were fairly well catered for, because of legacies which had come to their mother and because of a Trust created before the death of Thomas, over of some of the Thornton land. Indirectly this Trust would have a beneficial effect on Methodism in Thornton. Of the four children not referred to in detail, Peggy and Ellen were to remain spinsters, whilst Isabelle became the wife of Thomas Barton of Thornton and gave birth to thirteen children, and Gaskell married Thomas Bond of Out Rawcliffe. Both the last two families had some of their children baptized by Methodist Preachers and in the Bond's case a note to this effect was specially entered into the Parish Register of Hambleton. (9)

It is now over one hundred years since John Taylor wrote his book 'The Apostles of

71

Fylde Methodism', and in it you will find that there is no reference to the Gaskell family; but, as he points out in the preface of his book, he was not writing a history of Fylde Methodism but was presenting a number of biographical sketches about men and women who helped its advancement. Whereas the above information about the Gaskell family has come solely from documentary sources, Taylor was able to use the traditions and personal reminiscences of people who had knowledge of those about whom he wrote and their contemporaries. Such memories, whilst sometimes romanticized or even incorrect, are unique and usually unavailable from any other source, and tell of happenings and impressions from a much more human standpoint than any document could. Betty Tomlinson was one of those people remembered.

Betty was born in 1775, the daughter of Thomas and Nanny Greenwood of Thornton and when she was in her early twenties she married John Thomason (not Tomlinson), who became a butcher in Poulton. Following her conversion, which occurred one day when she was praying in solitude in some form of a shelter used by the cattle, she began meeting regularly with other like-minded women in a prayer meeting, much to the chagrin of her husband. In the hope of curing her of these praying habits he locked her out of the house on occasions, but to no avail. Then he began to suspect that they were meeting for something other than prayer, so he decided to find out. He was able to conceal himself in the place where they were meeting, hoping to confirm his suspicions, but he was surprised in a way other than what he had expected, for at one point their prayers were offered on his behalf. They asked that his heart might be changed and for God to make him a new creature. Conscience stricken he came out of his hiding place and answered their prayers by pleading for forgiveness, and from then on he gave devoted service to the Society and Methodism, and eventually became a leader. He was the one who drove Moses Holden to Thornton in his shandry.

On that occasion Holden probably preached at the house of Thomas and Nanny Greenwood, which had been available for preaching since January 1809. (10) Their humble cottage, which stood next to the Thornton Mill was the centre of the cause, and it was here that meetings were generally held, together with the occasional preaching service. John Taylor records that it was from this cottage that their son William went to Darwen to start Methodism there. William, as has been indicated, was already settled in that place with his wife, when he was influenced by William Banning to start his class meting in 1789 at Blackburn, so could the reverse have been the case, with William inspiring his parents to open up their cottage for the Methodists?

It was at this cottage that some young pranksters once climbed onto the roof and dropped a goose down the chimney, whilst a prayer meeting was being held. As it fell it swept the chimney with it beating wings and brought down soot and smoke into the room as it landed on the hearth and interrupted the meeting, which was the intention. Apparently, although frightened, it was none the worse for its descent, so the meeting continued as it settled down amongst them, squatting peacefully at their feet until the proceedings were over. The members themselves were not averse to a little mischief, and often teased Holden. In his diary he records, "I was often sorely tried with the people at Thornton Marsh. They took it into their heads that I must be proud, because I always had a good coat on my back; and so they would try to humble me....They told me afterwards that they had done it to try me". (11)

Nevertheless, Holden's preaching and influence must have had an effect on the members at Thornton, for by their industry and the goodwill of friends they were able to build themselves a chapel within eighteen months of his leaving. In this connection Ellen Dagger and her family once again demonstrated their devotion to Methodism. Under the Thornton Marsh Enclosure Award an allotment of land was awarded to the Daggers in respect of that Thornton land held under the Trust which had been created by Thomas Dagger, and in November 1812 a portion of this allotment was sold to the Thornton Society in order that a chapel could be built on it. This was quickly done and reputedly opened the same year. The actual Deed of Conveyance to the Trustees of the chapel was only completed on 16th April 1813 and was entered into by Ellen Dagger, her three married daughters and their husbands and also her two spinster daughters, Margaret and Ellen. The description of the property reads, "...a plot of land in Thornton, bounded on the west by land of Richard Broadbelt, and on the south by a lane, containing 238 square yards...together with a chapel lately erected..."; then follows this unusual clause, "except the occupiers of the land adjacent to the East gable wall can build against the wall for support.... and the occupiers of the land on the North can take rainwater off the chapel in vats". (12)

From this description it can therefore be deduced that the chapel abutted both the north and east boundaries of the plot. Fortunately there is a photograph of this old chapel which has been preserved, showing it as it was in its latter days. It was a plain barn-like structure whose length ran from east to west, with an entrance door near to the south west corner of the building. There was a small piece of ground, slightly elevated, fronting the chapel, and this was surrounded by railings and a gate leading from the lane, then known as Ramper Road. The chapel cost £150.

Witnessing the Conveyance were four Methodist preachers, John Thomason from Poulton and John Bleasdale, a tailor of Thornton Marsh. The latter had been born in 1788, son of James and Jane, and he eventually became the leader of the Society and one of the subsequent Trustees. An examination of the original Trustees shows that the influence of Preston Methodism was still strong, despite not then being in the Preston Circuit, from which it had earlier received support. There were three Trustees who came from there; Thomas Threlfall (linen draper), Robert Park (ironmonger), and Richard Parkinson (joiner). The remaining Trustees were Richard Knagg of Garstang (mole catcher), William Bell Threlfall of Pilling (Yeoman), James Roskell and Richard

Charnley of Thornton (Yeomen). Some of the others who were part of the early fellowship at Thornton were Richard and Mary Bryning, Samuel and Mary Linley, John Charnley, Ben Wilding and Mrs. Betty Charnley, but the inspiration and leadership came from James Roskell, who had been converted before he settled in Thornton.

James was born at Bispham in 1775, son of the wheelwright Richard and his wife Ellen, formerly Hull. When he was only six years old his father died and for eleven more years Ellen was left to bring up James, his sister Mary and two others until she married again in 1793, this time to a John Fare. For a few years nothing further is known of James until, sometime at the beginning of the Nineteenth Century he enlisted in the army and eventually was fighting in the Peninsular War, where he received a bayonet wound on his cheek. He must have only served in that war for a short period, because by January 1809 he was established in Thornton, and this was after spending some time in Ireland, at Clonmel, County Tipperary. There, whilst most of the soldiers spent their time drinking and gambling, James and a few others were befriended by a small group of Methodists, who invited them to their fellowship. As a result a few of these soldiers, including James, were converted and from then on they created a place for themselves in their barracks, where they could meet together. Although they were opposed by the more unruly and had to suffer insults, as well as attempts at eviction from their quarters, their commanding officer intervened and they were granted the right to meet in peace. Whilst there each of them obtained a leather bound pocket bible, and eventually James's copy was to become a treasured possession of his family in Blackpool long after his death. (13) His discharge from the army must have occurred soon after these events. Possibly his settling in Thornton could have had something to do with the resurgence of Methodism there, and also the dedication of Greenwood's cottage, for which James was a petitioner.

His sister Mary was married in 1808 to John Hodgson, alias Whiteside, and they went to live at Little Layton, where he owned about thirty five acres, as well as a couple of cottages in the village. Here their three children, Ellen (1809), John (1811) and Richard (1813) were born, but by 1816 Mary was a widow. Very soon her brother James, who was an executor for her husband, went to live with Mary and her family at Little Layton, where they stayed for a couple of years before moving to Out Rawcliffe. Despite this moving around the links that James had with the Thornton Society were not broken. Whilst living across the river Wyre he would take the ferry from Hambleton, carrying his lunch with him in order that he could still lead his class, before returning home in time to do the milking. Gradually, however, he began to see that the work at Thornton was progressing sufficiently for him to hand over the leadership so that he could concentrate on helping with a Society on his side of the river. Consequently his friend, John Bleasdale, took over from him, leaving James to devote his energies with the people at Out Rawcliffe.

During the second decade of the nineteenth century the Poulton Society continued to meet in its warehouse premises, which by then had passed to Thomas Barton under the terms of John Gaskell's will, but not everything went smoothly for them. Whilst they were there they had to endure some abuse and insults from those who had developed a prejudice against them. On one occasion an unruly mob broke into the meeting room, smashed all the windows and dragged the pulpit into the Market Place, hinting that since they were Methodists they had no need of a place of worship seeing that much of their preaching was done outdoors.

Apart from the problems which occur amongst certain sections in Northern Ireland, religious intolerance in our modern day society seems to have given way to a more liberal attitude and even indifference as to the way people express their beliefs. As a result it is not easy to understand how such intolerance affected the lives of people living and working in a village such as Poulton. Apart from the occasional outburst by one or other of the more narrow minded clergy in the vicinity, as well as the unruliness of some of the rougher element in the community, it is doubtful if Poulton experienced more than a minor disturbance because of the way people chose to worship. Many of those who were connected with Methodism seem to have come from a respectable section of the community or they were engaged in trade, and as such would tend to cultivate a friendly relationship with their neighbours.

The first membership returns in 1815 show that the numbers who attended Class Meetings had little altered since Holden's visit, but as in other places mentioned, there would be others less committed who would attend on other occasions. (14) The names of the people found in the returns are - John and Betty Thomason, Ellen Fare, Margaret Campbell, Ellen Dagger, Thomas Hodskinson, William and Betty Malley, Ellen Smith, Jane Fare, Betty Greenwood and Francis Dennison. Within two years only the first six named were still in membership, but by then twenty more had been added. Because of the growth consideration began to be given to the necessity of obtaining a more permanent place in which to worship. This led to a Subscription List being started towards a Building Fund. By 1819 the response was sufficient enough for them to consider the next step, and a site, at the lower end of Back Street (Chapel Street) near its junction with Green Street (Queen Square), was purchased from a W. Cross. A thatched cottage at this corner, tenanted by James Singleton, was included in the purchase price. Building commenced soon after and by November that year a chapel had been built. This was erected at the north end of the plot set back slightly from the street; a simple construction of brick and timber with a slate roof, but an earthen floor. Furnishings included seating, a coalstove, a chandelier for the candles, pulpit furniture, a bible and hymn book, and probably a clock. The total cost of the land and cottage, which needed repairs, the building of the chapel by Thomas Seed, the furnishings and other expenses came to almost £375. Included in these costs were several entries relating to something which later Methodists would have looked at in aghast, for they were for the payment of thirty three and a half quarts of ale consumed by the building workers, plus a small quantity of liquor. As only £123 had been raised through donations and collections etc., the members were grateful for a loan of £200 which was made available by a Mrs. Hodgson. (15)

Over the years both the Seed and Hodgson families gave sterling service to the Society at Poulton, and the families became united through marriage. Thomas Seed and his wife Mary had become members of the Society by 1817 when Thomas became leader of one of the classes, the other being John Thomason. The former came from a large Skippool family of flaggers and slaters, who had been living in the area for over a hundred years. His father, Richard, was one who often used the then port of Skippool to import coal and slate. Not long after building the chapel the family removed to the Manchester area for a few years but by 1830 they had returned to Poulton and they renewed their membership in the Society. Their son Richard also served faithfully after becoming a member. He was probably influenced by what became known as the Great Revival in Poulton, which lasted over a couple of years from 1830. This helped to increase the membership to sixty one by the Spring of 1832. The total population of Poulton Township in 1831 was 1025 with approximately 559 of them estimated to have been aged twenty or over. (16) Thus even allowing for a few members being under that age and some being outsiders the 1832 membership would be approaching ten per cent of the adult population. This of course does not take into consideration those who were connected in some way, but had not made any commitment.

Included in the 1832 list of members is the name of Catherine Lewtas, who three years later was to marry Richard Seed. (17) She was the youngest daughter of George Lewtas, a carpenter of Poulton, and his wife Mary, whose brother Henry Banks has been referred to as the 'Father of Blackpool'. Early in 1830 when the Great Revival was beginning Catherine had a conversion experience and from then on spent her life, in conjunction with her husband, in supporting and promoting Methodism in the area, despite an accident encountered by Richard in giving service. Richard made a practice of assisting the preachers who were appointed locally and also to the new Society which had been formed at Blackpool in 1832, by providing them with transport if necessary from Poulton in his horse and trap. On the occasions when he went to Blackpool it is reported that he took with him a duster and candles, to ensure that the place was clean and had sufficient light. These trips, however, became less frequent when the railway was extended to the resort in 1846, but he still continued to transport preachers elsewhere. It was whilst he was on such a journey with a preacher, Garstang bound, that an accident occurred not too far from his home in Breck Street, when his horse fell and overturned the trap. This resulted in Richard severely breaking his leg and which eventually necessitated having to have it amputated below the knee, thus handicapping him for the remainder of his life. This occurred sometime after he had erected the first Methodist chapel in Blackpool in 1835, emulating what his father had previously done in Poulton. He was also involved with other building work in Blackpool, one area being at Larkhill just to the south of the present railway station, where his name is remembered by having a street named after him. Both Catherine and Richard lived in Poulton all their life together, before she died in 1867, followed by him fifteen years later. Their family grave has a prominent position alongside the path leading to the south door of the Parish Church. A newspaper report at the time of Richard's death stated that he would be sadly missed. (18) When Catherine Lewtas was first converted in 1830 she was regarded as somewhat of a curiosity by her older married sister, Jane Hodgson, but before the end of the year she too had changed her way of life and joined the Poulton Society. Unfortunately she only survived another nineteen months but despite a period of painful affliction she did not give up her faith, and was often to be found distributing religious tracts. The Lewtas conversions, however, did not stop with Jane, for about the same time a George Lewtas, probably their father, who despite his advancing years also became united in the same fellowship. (19)

The Hodgsons were fairly widespread throughout this part of the Fylde and a branch of the family had been at Warbreck at least since Elizabethan times and became strong Presbyterians. George, who was born there, had been baptized by a Presbyterian minister in 1730, but he eventually settled in Poulton as a skinner. One of his sons, William, was to marry Mary Parkinson and they had several offspring amongst whom was one also called William, later the spouse of Jane Lewtas. William Junior also carried on the business of a skinner and fellmonger from Sheaf Street, whilst his three younger brothers, John, Henry and Thomas, ran an ironmongery and grocery shop in Market Place. Their nonconformity was now expressed in serving Methodism at Poulton and elsewhere, with William and John becoming Trustees of the Blackpool and Thornton chapels. Two of the daughters of William and Jane also married local Methodists, Mary, a schoolmistress, to John Stirzaker and Margaret to Robert, son of Braithwaite and Margaret Bond, who had been members since 1819. When William Hodgson died in 1875, Robert and Margaret's son inherited his grandfather's estate on condition that he changed his name from Bond to Hodgson. This he did and eventually became the first chairman of Poulton Urban District Council, then chairman of the Lancashire County Council after becoming Sir William Hodgson. By then this branch of the family was no longer Methodist.

At the time of the Great Revival some of those who had been associated with early Poulton Methodism had passed on. Ellen Dagger died in 1823, but her name was remembered and appeared regularly in the accounts of the Trustees of the chapel until 1854 because of a loan made to the chapel from her estate. (20) Her brother, Thomas Gaskell, also died in the same year at Stalmine with Staynall, where he had been leader of a small Society until just prior to his death. (21) One of his contemporaries, Robert Harrison, whose house had been used as a meeting place in the previous century moved to be with his son at Liverpool in 1825 and died there three years later.

Some of the other older members were still giving service. The Thomasons continued in membership with John still leader of one of the classes, of which there were now four. James Roskell was also a leader having moved from Out Rawcliffe, as was Lawrence Disley. The latter, formerly of Salwick, had moved to Poulton by 1807 when he was married to Nanny Greenwood at Poulton Parish Church. They lived in a few places over the next ten years, including a period as a tenant of Thomas Gaskell at Out Rawcliffe, but finally returned to Poulton where Lawrence was found to be a member after the death of his wife. Eventually in 1836 he was employed as caretaker of the chapel for a few years and moved into the chapel cottage. He remained in Poulton the rest of his life. The allegiance to Methodism was continued through his son in law James Edgar, who served thirty five years as a minister with the Protestant Methodists until his death in 1867. Others joining the Society at the same time as Disley were Edmund and Elizabeth Thornton - he ran the smithy at Carleton for over forty years - the Carter family of Bull Street, where Richard was a glazier, Richard Parkinson, and members of the Smith family.

Richard Parkinson was a merchant, corn miller and maltster, whose surname would later become synonymous with Methodism locally and in the business affairs of the town. He was one of the Chapel Stewards and a trustee for both the Thornton and Blackpool chapels. His wife was none other than the former Ellen Whitehead - the first Poultonian recorded in the Preston baptismal register. James Smith was the leader of the fourth class in 1832 and both he and his brother Edward, who were tailors, became Local Preachers in the Garstang Circuit.

The Revival also inspired other young men to take up the challenge of preaching. One was Robert Crookall, a cordwainer, who was to marry Ellen Hodgson, the niece of James Roskell, in 1835 and then move to Little Layton, where her parents had farmed. From there they began attending the chapel that had just been erected at Blackpool, about which some reference will later be made. George Singleton, a joiner of Back Street, was another who began to preach. He was reputed to be the first person to preach in the meeting room of the Fleetwood Society when it was founded about 1838. Finally there was John Stirzaker, son of Richard - a wheelwright of Tithebarn Street, and his wife Ellen. John was seventeen when he was converted but his mother was opposed to it and used to prevent him from attending class meetings, sometimes by locking him in his bedroom. There was one occasion when he escaped her clutches and had gone to the chapel, but along came his mother and dragged him from out of the service and gave him a good hiding; but it was to no avail. Years later someone wrote about this part of his life and stated '....in face of much domestic opposition he united himself to the people amongst whom he had learned the way of the Lord'. He learned well and soon became a Local Preacher, before eventually entering the Methodist ministry in 1838. Apparently by this time his mother had overcome her bigotry for she allowed herself to hear him preach whenever he visited Poulton. His pulpit talents were

78

reported to be of a superior order, with his sermons lucid and instructive. He married Mary Hodgson, one of the daughters of William and Jane, but she only survived a few years until November 1845. John served in various Circuits, mainly in the North of England and Scotland for sixteen years, before having to give up because of ill health. He died in March 1854, aged forty two, and was buried at Admaston, Shropshire. He was the first known local person to enter the Methodist ministry. (22)

Thornton's first chapel at Ramper Road (Victoria Road).

Chapter Nine

The Western Horizon

Whilst Methodism began to flourish and grow in Thornton and Poulton, at the nearby resort of Blackpool the introduction of a place of worship was very slow in coming. Writing in 1837 Rev. William Thornber, Blackpool's first historian, lamented the fact that near the end of the Eighteenth Century an attempt to erect an Established Church in the town had failed dismally, with but £100 being subscribed to the project. (1) Earlier in 1788 William Hutton made similar comments and added "....there is not even a Methodist rearing against the wall", (2) Following this it was over thirty years before St. John's was opened as an episcopal chapel in the Parish of Bispham to provide the spiritual needs of those living in Blackpool. At that time, as the town was beginning to develop during the summer months, due to the increase of visitors frequenting the resort, those who were Methodists did not have any place in which to worship and if they wished to attend a Methodist service they could only be satisfied by travelling the four miles to the chapel at Poulton.

More than a decade was to further pass before Methodism eventually took root in the town. Once again James Roskell appeared on the scene, having left Poulton to return to Little Layton where his sister Mary was living, after having then married John Dobson. James, with his usual missionary zeal, decided that there was a need which had to be attended to. Towards the summer of 1832 he enlisted the help of Robert Baird, an Irishman by birth but then of Preston, where he had a drapery business. He also ran a branch of this business in Blackpool during the summer months. The two men were able to acquire the use of a room at Bonny's Bathing House at the sea end of Bonny's Lane (now Chapel St.). Here a small group began to hold their meetings and during the busier summer months their numbers were swelled by the Methodist visitors on holiday. One of these early visitors to Bonny's was William Heap of Halifax, who had been visiting the resort for several years and who was one of those making the journey to the Poulton chapel. (3) He was to continue attending the Blackpool Society for many years after and eventually was to have the honour of laying a foundation stone for the 1862 chapel at Hound's Hill. The Blackpool meeting was at first not linked to the Garstang Circuit, but support was given by some preachers from Preston, amongst whom were the temperance advocates connected with Methodism there, much to the annoyance of Thornber, then the curate at St. John's, who threatened them with loss of their preaching licence.

The evangelistic work started by the two men soon came to be recognized, however, for at a Local Preacher's meeting held at Garstang on 24th September 1832 the Society became part of that Circuit and it was resolved "....Blackpool shall be tried once a month as a preaching place; services to be held at six o'clock on Sunday evening". (4) During the following months the Circuit was encouraged by the progress in the town. With the increase of summer visitors the room at the Bathing House soon became too small, so meetings were transferred to Robert Baird's Bazaar, close to the site of the future chapel. Robert held two properties in a terrace on the south side of a small street, which came to be known as Heywood Street, after Sir Benjamin Heywood whose house 'West Hey' was built on the site of the future Tower. One of the properties, Wellington Cottage, was used by Baird and his family, whilst adjoining was his drapery bazaar fronting Bank Hey Street. (5) Almost two years later there were further developments when a special Circuit meeting comprised of representatives from Scorton, Preston and Garstang, together with William and John Hodgson and Richard Parkinson from Poulton, was convened to discuss the possibility of erecting a chapel at Blackpool, and also the measures that would be needed to obtain the necessary funds.(6) It was felt that because of the peculiar circumstances surrounding a 'resort' chapel, where there was need for greatly increased accommodation for worshippers during the holiday season, but yet only token support locally at other times, it should be financed from a much wider area than normal, and in the hope that this would be so they sought to appoint Trustees from among the prominent Methodists in various parts of Lancashire and the West Riding of Yorkshire. This was no doubt deemed to be suitable because it was from these areas that the bulk of the summer visitors came.

The response cannot have been what had been hoped for, because only four of them accepted the responsibility, with the other nineteen Trustees having to be found from either Preston or the Garstang Circuit. Consequently all the eleven laymen who were at the special Circuit meeting were obliged to accept this duty. Prominent also in the list from Preston was the name of Robert Baird. (7) Once the Trustees had been found the task of appealing for subscriptions was then undertaken, for it had been decided that until sufficient funds had been received the chapel should not be built. Letters requesting support were sent out over a wide area and personal solicitations were made for donations to the cause, especially in Preston where the work was done by Thomas Crouch Hincksman. By the Spring of 1835 the response had been such that the project could go ahead.

The first step was the purchase on 13th May that year of a freehold site 39 x 20 yards from land belonging to the Hull Estate. (8) The plot lay immediately behind the Royal Hotel and the terrace where Baird had his bazaar, and also adjoined a group of cottages owned by James Caunce, which had recently been built on the south side. The consideration was £58.10.-. Shortly after this, sanction was given for the erection of a chapel at a cost of £360.-. and work was quickly started and completed within a couple of months. The building was probably opened for worship in October, for future Anniversary Services were celebrated in that month. It was an unpretentious building of 45' x 39', built with plain brick by Richard Seed of Poulton chapel. It did not have a balcony but yet it was reported to be able to accommodate about 250 people in fixed high back pews. It was planned that seat rents totalling £20 per annum. were to be charged in order to defray the cost of heating and lighting. (9) It is doubtful if very much was raised this way by the local members for in 1835 prior to the chapel being built there were only ten of them in Blackpool and Marton. At Poulton the year before, when membership was in the region of fifty, only £13.12.-. was raised in seat rents.

Developments were also taking place in the area of the chapel. In addition to the road which passed between the chapel and the Royal Hotel site (now Bank Hey Street), a lane had been created on the north side, to which the chapel fronted, leading inland from the sea, first known as Chapel Lane, but then when it was opened out as Upper Adelaide Street. The chapel was near to what is the entrance of the present Central Methodist Church. Besides the cottages which stood to the south another one had been built to the east by John Braithwaite, known as Greenfield Cottage, which much later was occupied by the chapel caretaker before it was eventually absorbed in extensions to the chapel. (10)

About the same time that Methodism was being introduced to Blackpool, it was also making a re-appearance at Marton. Moses Holden had reported that there was a Society there in 1811 with a total of seven members, but this seems to have faded away. During the intervening years the name does not appear in the records of either the Preston or Garstang Circuits, although a Society was formed in the latter Circuit at neighbouring Weeton in 1822 and was probably having meetings four years earlier. (11) It was still functioning when Marton revived. Credit for the re-awakening was due to John and Jane Bennett who had opened up their home at Runnell Farm, Moss Side for preaching services by 1833, having moved there from Out Rawcliffe. It was whilst they were at the latter place that they had been introduced to Methodism and had become members of that Society in 1826, under the leadership of none other than James Roskell, little realizing that a few years later he would be their leader in a combined Blackpool and Marton class. (12) By 1838, however, the Bennett's had moved again - this time to Blackpool, where they took the tenancy of Foxhall Farm for a few years. (13) Blackpool's gain was Marton's loss, resulting in an interruption of the work there until it was revived by John Hall, who began to hold meetings at his house at Stockydale Road prior to the building of the Blowing Sands chapel in 1847. (14)

The work at Blackpool continued under the leadership of the founders, with Robert Baird increasingly spending more time in the town, until he eventually came to live permanently at the cottage adjoining his business. Roskell, however, was a restless type of a person who never seemed to stay in one place for any length of time. His guidance and leadership were so valuable to those early Societies, but it appears that when he felt his work was complete he would move on. This was the case at Blackpool, for before 1841 he had moved to Fleetwood, where he lived in near poverty because of his generosity to some poorer than himself. (15) His name does not appear in any of the earlier references to Fleetwood Methodism, which commenced about 1838, but it is inconceivable to think that he would not have given his support to it. He did not look upon himself as being poor, for just before he died he told his old friend John Bleasdale, whom he had served with at Thornton and who often used to visit him, "The Lord is good to me.....I've just enough" He lies somewhere in an unknown grave. (16)

Baird was the driving force in the running of the Sunday School which had been started at Blackpool and his concern for the young people was paramount, supporting the work financially as well as providing leadership. A few years after the school had been established the then incumbent of St. John's Church began to take up an attitude of intolerance towards the Methodists and others, which eventually caused some reaction. Some of the Bennett children who were members of the Methodist Sunday School also attended the St. John Day School in Church Street. This school had opened as a National School in 1817 but came to be known by the name of St. John, "although at that time it had no connection with the later church of the same name and was free to all denominations". The Trust Deed of February 1820 laid out the curriculum and this again inferred that children of parents not belonging to the Church of England were entitled to attend. Three of the Trustees had been appointed in perpetuity; the Patron of the Living of Bispham, the Rector of Bispham and the Vicar of Marton. Whether they had any influence on what was to follow is unknown, but the curate of St. John's Church declared that no child in the future would be allowed to attend the Day School if they did not also attend his Sunday School and Church. This of course affected the Bennett children, who continued to attend the Sunday School at Hound's Hill. Consequently they were discouraged from attending the Day School. Clearly a display of religious intolerance. (17)

The directive caused Robert Baird to act, and with characteristic nerve and audacity he declared that the Wesleyan Methodists would have a Day School of their own. He therefore called a meeting to which he invited friends and supporters, and explained to them the circumstances which had brought it about and presented to them his ideas for the creation of a Wesleyan Day School. The plans met with the meeting's approval and very quickly a school was established and it began to meet in the room situated at the rear of the chapel. In the early period of its existence the pupils were taught by Robert Bond, son of Braithwaite Bond of Poulton, and who was a few years later the father of the child destined to become Sir William Hodgson. William Mason succeeded Bond for a few years and then in 1851 a young man of twenty, William Parkinson Wesley, who was later to become the founder of Moor Park Academy, Preston, and associated with the North Road Wesleyan Chapel, served in the post. (18) Space must have been at a premium at that time, for in the following year a new school was erected to the west of the chapel and fronting to Bank Hey Street. Apparently, although done with good intentions, construction was undertaken without the official approval of the Wesleyan Chapel Trustees, as future events were to reveal. (19) That the Trustees should have allowed the buildings to go ahead on the face of it seems unusual, but by this time some

83

of the original Trustees had died and some of those who lived out of town probably did not realize what was taking place, but that did not excuse those who were well aware of the situation. Robert Baird, who had been the father figure in the Sunday School and the only trustee who lived in Blackpool, had passed away in January 1850. (20)

A Blackpool School Building Committee had been formed, which authorised T. Drummond, builder, to erect the school on the chapel land under contract at a cost of £220, which was also to include the fitting up of the inside of the building, obviously unaware that they were not empowered to act in this way. To meet the cost of the building, subscriptions were solicited between June and August that year totalling £133-9.-, leaving a shortfall of £86.11.-. which seems to have been borrowed. The subscription list proves interesting reading with most of the donors being known Methodists, and included William Heap of Halifax, Francis Parnell, then of Manchester but later the benefactor of Rawcliffe Street chapel and one of Blackpool's mayors, George Fishwick, millowner of Scorton and son in law of Roger Crane, Robert Curwen, Treasurer of the Building Committee, and John Wignall, shipowner of Fleetwood. Other small cash donations were collected by Robert Crookall. (21)

The latter was one who had been converted in the Great Revival at Poulton, following which he married James Roskell's niece Ellen Hodgson. When the latter's younger brother Richard died at Charlestown, U.S.A. she came into the possession of about ten acres of land near to the Convent, as well as a house, two cottages and a small plot in the centre of Little Layton village, where she went to live with her new husband about the time that the Blackpool chapel was being opened. Their eldest son Richard was baptized by the Circuit minister in September 1836, the first in Blackpool. (22) By 1856 he had become the schoolteacher at the Wesleyan Day School, succeeding William D. Read, who had followed Wesley. Very soon though matters came to a head regarding the use of the school and its accountability. On 24 January 1857 a Special Meeting of the then surviving Blackpool Wesleyan Trustees was held at Lune Street, Preston, where several resolutions were passed, which provided some details of the situation but which also created more mystery. (23)

Notice was given to Richard Crookall that his occupancy of the school building must cease by the end of the following month and the key left with the Rev. Ben Gartside, the minister of the chapel and then Superintendent of the Circuit. Crookall was also advised that as from 2nd March he could rent the chapel vestry as a schoolroom for the peppercorn rent of 1/- per annum, which was to be kept in proper repair and be clean for all meetings and classes. On the same day Rev. Gartside, Thomas Hincksman and Henry Threlfall, the latter being Trustees, were to take possession of the school building. The Trustees were to pay Robert Curwen the balance still due to him as Treasurer of the School Committee, together with interest since the debt had been created. Application was to be then made to the Chapel Building Committee of the

Wesleyan Methodist Church to place the schoolroom, together with a debt of £100 on the Local Trust.

Richard Crookall did not take up the offer of renting the chapel vestry for a Day School, which resulted in its demise. Many years later there was criticism directed against these Trustees for unwisely closing the school, but obviously they were unaware of the problems at that time. Richard shortly afterwards joined the Congregational Church and entered its ministry and by 1862 had commenced a three year pastorate at Tockholes. Once the school was safely in the hands of the Trustees they generated an income from it by renting it out for various events in the town to help reduce the debt that had been created.

The Special Trustees Meeting also passed a resolution that Robert Crookall was to give up his Chapel Steward's book by 6th February and give a statement of all the monies received and paid since 30th April of the previous year to Rev. Gartside, who was appointed Chapel Steward in his place. This was an unusual appointment for a minister, but he was given the power to have Assistant Stewards who were to account to him for all the collections and have them properly recorded. Apparently since student preachers were being supplied weekly during the summer months, Sabbath collections were always taken, but seat rents were to be considered during the other months. Thanks were expressed to George Parkinson for his services as Treasurer of the chapel and it was resolved that he be re-appointed. The salary and duties of the Chapel Keeper were from then on to be dealt with by the minister and Henry Threlfall. (24)

No reason was given for asking Robert Crookall to give up his position as Chapel Steward, but undoubtedly it had something to do with the operation of the Day School and the duties of the caretaker. It has been shown that he was instrumental in 1852 for collecting many small cash gifts and in his official capacity he would also be the person with whom the School Committee would have contact regarding the use and running of the school premises. It would seem that he had overstepped his authority or had been careless in some of his financial affairs. There were other occasions when, acting in his capacity as the town's Tax Collector, he was questioned regarding the overtaxing of some of the property owners. None of the incidents seem to have blotted his character in any way, either at the chapel or in the town, for he was considered suitable to be appointed as a Trustee for Thornton Chapel in 1869 and he continued as Tax collector for the town until his death in 1875, after serving in the position for thirty years. He and some of his family were still connected with the Blackpool Chapel over the ensuing years, and he still continued as a Local Preacher, and attended the Quarterly Meetings.

Over the years the Society at Blackpool had grown and at times during the season only about one third of those wishing to do so could get in the chapel. It also grew in importance, for in September 1856 Blackpool became the head of a Circuit in place of

Garstang, and it was known as the Blackpool and Garstang Circuit. Up to this date the Superintendent Minister had resided in the latter place, with the other two Circuit ministers being stationed at Fleetwood and Poulton, but in that year Poulton lost its resident minister when Rev. Benjamin Gartside was appointed Superintendent and went to live at 3 Adelaide Street, Blackpool. (25)

Meanwhile, the nearby Greenfield Cottage had been put up for sale in August 1855 by the Braithwaite family. Although very desirable the Trustees felt that they were not in a position to purchase the property, but on 1 May 1857 it was obtained by one who was connected with Methodism elsewhere in the Circuit and then let out to the Trustees. The new owner was John Armer, a schoolmaster of Churchtown and also a Local Preacher. A letter of his is still extant dated 29th September 1859, which was sent to the Trustees advising them that he would be willing to sell the cottage provided that a satisfactory agreement was drawn up, allowing him to lease back the property for the term of his life and that of another, subject to an annual payment. Failing this he would retain the cottage until his death, when it would go to the highest bidder. The Trustees did not take up his offer, but did, however, continue to rent it until they were able to purchase it in 1865. (26)

Rev. Gartside stayed at Blackpool for three years and to the latter part of his term more and more people could see that there was a need for a larger building. In 1859 he became a Supernumary and retired to Poulton to live; but that was not the end of his work for the Blackpool Chapel. He was succeeded by Rev. E. Oldfield, and it was during his ministry that the discussions and planning of a new chapel took off in earnest. Gartside, however, now being free from his circuit duties was able to give much of his time to the new venture and wrote countless numbers of letters to those he thought would be sympathetic in contributing to the costs. Besides writing to those who were summer visitors to the Blackpool Chapel, he also wrote to his friends and contacts in other Circuits. There was also a need to appoint new Trustees, so beside appealing for funds and subscriptions, he also contacted those he thought would be willing to take on such a responsibility. One of the first letters which he wrote in the spring of 1860 in this connection was to Francis Parnell Esq., then of Cheetham, Manchester. The reply from Mr. Parnell was a promise of £50 towards the cause, but he declined to become a Trustee. At that time he little realised that in just over five years time he would have reason to settle in South Shore and become worker and principal benefactor to the Rawcliffe Street Chapel there. (27)

Two other people to whom Rev. Gartside wrote were F.W.Heaton of Bolton and William Mewburn of Halifax, who in turn collected gifts and subscriptions from their friends and acquaintances. That there was a need for a larger building was obvious, for during the summer of 1860 some of the services were being held in the school, and collections were taken in order to defray the expense of having to fit up the room for

GARSTANG AND BLACKPOOL CIRCUIT.

SABBATH DAY AND WEEK EVENING
APPOINTMENTS,
FROM AUGUST 3rd, TO NOVEMBER 30th, 1856.

"But they that wait upon the Lord shall renew their strength; they shall mount up with wings as eagles; they shall run, and not be weary; and they shall walk, and not faint." Isa. xl. 31.

"That I might by all means save some." 1 Cor. ix. 22.

PLACES & TIME.		AUGUST.				SEPTEMBER.				OCTOBER.				NOVEMBER.			
		3	10	17	24	31	7	14	21	28	5	12	19	26	2	9	16	23	30
GARSTANG ....10½, 6½ Thursday 7½		2 28 3	11 8	13 10 3	6 6	1 1 3T	9 18	2Q 3Q 3T	13 12 3	3 3	5 5 3	1 1S 3	4 4	2K 2K 3	17 8	9 10 3	4 11	1 1 3	18 18
SCORTON ....10½, 6½ Thursday 7½		5 6	21 21 2	4 18	1 1 3	28 28	2T 3S 1T	32 32	3Q 3Q 2	29 39	1L 1 3	10 11 1	2 3	33 33 2	3K 3K 3	23 23	1 1S 3	31 31	2 2 1T
HOLLINS LANE .. 2½		13	18	4	8	5	2T	11Q	10	13	1	8	5	6	3K	18	10	13	2
DOLPHINHOLME .. 2½, 6½ Wednesday 7		29 29	10 10 2	6 6 3	21 13	5 21 1T	34 5 2	3Q 34 3	28 10Q	11 28	18 18 1S	3 18 3	35 35	6K 6K 2	13 13 3	1 10 3	29 29 1	33 33
WOODPLUMPTON { 10½, 2½, 7 Monday 7		11 11 2	2 5	5 4 3	10 10	1S 6 1T	6 2Q 3	2Q 13	13 12 3	3 3 1	17 15	1 18 3	18 18	2K 2K	30 30 3	2 12 3	12 12	1 1T
GOOSNARGH 2½		36	40	38	15	27	17	37	2TQ	39	18	24	27	10	40	15	17K	11	1ST
BILSBORROW .10½, 2½ Tuesday 7		12 12	15 2S 2	11 11 3	5 5 3	18 18 1T	4 4Q 1T	9 9 2	6 6L	3 3 3	13 12	2 2S 3	17 17	2 2	15 11K 3	11K 8 3	8 5	5 4 3	4 4 1T
CATTERAL LANE 2½ Wednesday 7		2 3	11	13	9	1S 3	8	15Q	4	3	13	40	10	2	17 8K	11	1	15
CALDERVALE ...... 2½, 6, 7 Tuesday		18 18	17 17 3	40 40	11 11	6 6 3	10 10 3T	2Q 5Q 3T	8 8	4 4	9 9 3	1 13 3	17 17	11 11	18 18 5	5K 5K	40 40 3	10 10	8 8 1
BLACKPOOL ...10½, 6½ Tuesday 7 Friday 7½P		S 8 1 1	1 1 1 1	31 31 1 1	2 2 1 1	30 30 1 1	3 3 1T 1	8Q 8Q 1 1	8 1T 1	2 2S 1 1	1 25 1 1	25 25 1 1	3 3 1 1	16 16 1 1	1K 1K 1 1	20 20 1 1	2 2 1 1	17 17 1 1	3 3 1 1
TOULTON ...... 10½, 6½ Thursday 7		14 17	16 16	17 1S 1	27 20 1T	2 2 1	41 3Q 1	14 7 1	1 17 1	7 16 1	2 2 1	19 19 1	3 20 1	19 3 1	1K 20 1	14 7 1	14 2S 1	2 16 1	17 17 1
THORNTON .. 2 Wednesday 7		14	20	1	17 2T	2	12	3Q	14	18	17	3L 1	20	3	19 1	1K 3	14	2	17
BLOWING SANDS... 2½		S	1	7	2	16	3T	8Q	1	8	2S	7	3	12	1K	16	2	7	3
FLEETWOOD ...10½, 6½ Wed. & Day School 7		1 1 2	B B	2 2	35 35 2T	3Q 3Q	6 14 2	1S 1T 2	8 8	2 19	10 3	3 3	1 8 2	22 22 2	2K 2K	8 S 2	3 3	12 12
PILLING .... 2, 7 Monday 7		1 3	14	2 2 3	19 19 3T	3	6 2T	1QT 3	2Q 2	10 2	3	18	1	14 2	2K 19	19 3	3 3	10 2T
RAWCLIFFE .... 2, 7 Tuesday 7		20	41 3	12	18	4 2T	10Q	17	14	12	20	13	5 1	11 3	4K 41	19	9 2T	6
ECCLESTON ...... 10½, 2, 7 Monday 7		4 4	12 12 3	20 20 1	10 10	41 41 2T	11 9	9 5Q 3	5Q 17	17 14 3	14 14	4 6 2	6 20	20 10 3	3K 10 3	12 12	41 41 2T	9 9

Preachers' Names and Residences.

1 J. P. FAIRBOURN, Blackpool
2 J. MOORE, Fleetwood
3 E. COX, Garstang
4 J. ARMER, Churchtown
5 T. WILLS, Scorton
6 W. LANCASTER, Scorton
7 R. CROOKALL, Little Layton
8 G. WALKER, Garstang
9 J. FRYER, Catteral Lane
10 G. MAYOR, Garstang
11 G. WILLS, Scorton
12 R. THOMPSON, Thistleton
13 J. NUTTALL, Scorton
14 A. HOUGHTON, Pilling
15 T. WARD, Plumpton
16 J. HAYHURST, Blackpool
17 J. WESTWORTH, Plumpton
18 T. STANDEN, Scorton
19 A. GLEADHILL, Fleetwood
20 T. TOMLINSON

FROM OTHER CIRCUITS.

S. STUDENT, Didsbury
21 R. BOND, Lancaster
22 J. PARKINSON, Preston
23 W. HEATON, Do.
24 J. THRELFALL, Do.
25 W. WIGNALL, Kirkham
26 J. DARLINGTON, Preston
27 R. SALISBURY, Longridge
28 T. ROBERTS, Lancaster
29 — BOLTON, Do.
30 R. HARDMAN, Kirkham
31 W. P. WESLEY, Preston
32 F. BAYLISS, Do.
33 — BRADSHAW, Lancaster.
34 — DUGDALE, Do.
35 — PERCY, Do.
36 J. MOLINEUX, Preston
37 A. CLAYTON, do.
38 J. PEACOCK, do.
39 E. EWOOD, do.

EXHORTERS.

40 — BELL, Garstang
41 W. SWARBRICK, Poulton

NOTICES.

1.—THE QUARTERLY MEETING will be held at FLEETWOOD, on Monday, September 22nd, 1856. The Local Preachers to meet at TEN O'CLOCK, and the Stewards at HALF-PAST ELEVEN.

2.—The QUARTERLY FAST will be observed on Friday, October 3rd.

3.—Every Preacher is expected to fulfil his own appointments, or in case of inability, to get them supplied by an accredited substitute.

4.—The Society Stewards are requested to give notice of Sacraments, Lovefeasts, Weekly Services, and Collections, on the preceding Sunday; to see that the Collections are made according to the Plan; and to forward Connexional Funds, without delay, to the Superintendent Minister.

5.—Wesleyan Hymn Books, Magazines, and useful books of every description may be had of the Ministers.

REFERENCES.

S.S. Fleetwood Day School Sermons on Sunday, September 14th.
S. Sacrament.
L. Lovefeast.
Q. Quarterly Collection.

K. Collection for Kingswood and Woodhouse Grove Schools.
T. Renewal of Tickets.
P. Prayer Meeting.

this purpose. By then subscriptions had been promised from elsewhere in Lancashire and Yorkshire totalling £700 towards the new chapel. It was originally hoped to start building at the end of that season, but it was postponed for a further year.

By 1861 an application had been made on behalf of the Trustees by Thomas C. Hincksman, Thomas Threlfall and Edward Leece to the Chapel Committee for the new building, which was to seat 800 and to cost £2680. Sanction was duly given. Since the new chapel and also new vestries would occupy most of the site, the old chapel and the newer schoolroom had to be demolished before work could be completed, so it was arranged for this to be done after the summer. Consequently the last 'Sermons' to be held in the old building, and the twenty sixth since the opening, was on 17th October 1861, when the preacher was Thomas Hinksman. Friday, 1st November was arranged as a day of celebration for the laying of the corner stone by William Heap. Unfortunately when the day arrived the ceremony was dampened by inclement weather. Rain and occasional hail had been falling since early morning, resulting in the number attending the ceremony being much smaller than anticipated, so proceedings were begun in the old chapel, with Rev. Oldfield leading the service, assisted by Rev. David Hay, Superintendent of the Preston Circuit, and others. Rev. George Scott of Liverpool, the Chairman of the District, gave an address dwelling particularly on the doctrines and teachings of Methodism and the part the new chapel would have to play in this, and they concluded with the words of Wesley, "The best of all is God is with us". (28)

When the service was over the company reassembled outside for the remainder of the proceedings, where a platform had been built. After various items and papers had been placed in a bottle in the cavity beneath the corner stone, Mr. Heap performed the ceremony, tapping the stone with his mallet. He spoke to the gathering of how he had been a member of the Methodist Church for 62 years and had been in the habit of coming to Blackpool for the last forty one of them. He well remembered the beginnings of the Society in the bathing house and of the need to clean out the room in which they assembled, and also the building of the Day School. Thanking the Blackpool and other friends for the respect paid to him, he then declared the stone laid. Unfortunately, immediately after this had been completed the apparatus that had been used to lift the stone slipped and caused alarm to those nearby, but thankfully the wall of the school building prevented it from slipping any further and no one was injured. Some of the people, however, were shaken up, so the ceremony was quickly concluded; then off they went to partake of a dinner at the Clifton Arms Hotel, where various toasts and speeches were made.

Later in the day a further event was held. This was a Tea Meeting in Read's Assembly Rooms at South Beach (now Central Promenade); a building not then fully completed. Over 300 people sat down to the meal and many others arrived later for the meeting, at which Rev. Oldfield presented a financial statement and informed the assembly that up to that date there were donations and promises of £1781-17-6 and before the day was over it was hoped that £2000 would have been reached. Regrettably he had to announce that only £120-15-6 had been received from supporters at Blackpool and only £210 from elsewhere in the Circuit, which prompted him to remark that these paltry amounts were a condemnation of those who purported to support Methodism in the town and locally. The Chairman of the Meeting also expressed disappointment at the sum raised and hoped that before long the residents of Blackpool might increase the figure to £500.

It is not known when the last service was held in the old chapel, but it was demolished in January 1862 and services were transferred to Read's Assembly Rooms. Throughout the winter and spring, work proceeded on the new chapel and in a little over six months it was complete. The building was of classical design, contrasting sharply with the original one and covered twice as much floor space. The main entrance was approached by a few steps leading off Bank Hey Street into a lobby, from which access to the chapel could be gained either way to the ground floor or the stairs leading to the galleries at the rear of and along the sides of the chapel. The ground floor seating was for 500 in fixed pews, which were numbered and had doors to them, whilst the galleries were capable of accommodating 286 people. Behind the pulpit area was an organ gallery in an arched recess, but, although it had been planned for, there was at first no pipe organ. It would be a few years before one was installed and use had to be made of the seraphine harmonium, which had been purchased for the old chapel in 1858 at a cost of £12. [29] The new chapel was officially opened for services on Friday, 4th July 1862, when the special preacher was the Secretary of the Wesleyan Methodist Conference, Rev. John Farrer, and then there followed two weeks of special services conducted by eight guest preachers, in addition to Rev. Oldfield.

The opening of the new chapel gave Blackpool Methodism a firm foundation on which to build up the cause locally. All the preliminary work and enthusiasm prior to the building had generated more interest, but it was mainly newcomers to the town who helped swell the membership. This was perhaps only to be expected because of the rate the town itself was growing. In the decade following the erection of the chapel the resident population more than doubled; the town's first piers were built; a new planned estate was begun at North Shore; markets, assembly rooms, theatres and other entertainments were opened and the decade ended with the opening of a new promenade. All of this and more attracted an ever growing number of visitors whose needs had to be catered to; spiritual as well as social.

If it had been left solely to the indigenous population it is extremely unlikely that a new chapel would have been built. Only a few local families had stayed faithful since the early days - the Crookalls and Bennetts - and it has been shown that the financial support given locally was meagre. The future progress of Wesleyan Methodism was therefore mainly dependent on those who had been influenced elsewhere, before settling in the town. Because of them the subsequent years brought an expansion of the cause in the vicinity, but it was not all 'plain sailing' and they had to contend with some setbacks, as well as having to meet the challenge from the other branches of Methodism who were also establishing themselves.

They were also having to meet the challenge of a different age in a different type of society from that which had been encountered well over a century before by the early travelling preachers and the steadfast members. Whatever the task that lay ahead for them they could gain inspiration from the courage, devotion and perseverance shown by their predecessors.

Praise we the glorious names we know;
And they - whose names have perished,
Lost in the haze of long ago -
In silent love be cherished.

Reference Notes
and
Abbreviations used in the notes

Blackburn Book	Blackburn Circuit Cash Book, 1788-1816, held in the Archives at Wesley Hall, Blackburn.
Blackburn List	Blackburn Circuit List of Members, 1788-1808, held in the Archives at Wesley Hall, Blackburn.
BGN	Blackpool Gazette and News.
FC	Fleetwood Chronicle, Blackpool Herald and Lytham Gazette.
Haworth Book	Haworth Circuit Record Book from 1748, held at Keighley Library.
Haworth List	Haworth Circuit Membership Lists and Society Contributions, 1764-76, held at Keighley Library.
IGI	International Genealogical Index.
JBD	John Bennet's Diary, held at the Methodist Archive and Research Centre at John Rylands University Library, Manchester.
JCW	*Journal of Charles Wesley*, 2 Vols., Beacon Hill Press, Kansas City, (1980 reprint).
JWJ	*Journal of John Wesley*, 8 Vols., N. Curnock (Ed), Reprinted by Epworth Press, 1938. In view of various other editions of this work the Journal entry dates have been used in the reference notes.
LCWHS	Lancashire and Cheshire Wesley Historical Society.
Letters	*Letters of John Wesley*, 8 Vols., J.Telford (Ed), Epworth Press, 1931.
LRO	Lancashire Record Office, Bow Lane, Preston.
Minutes	Minutes of the Early Methodist Conferences, *Wesley Historical Society Publication I*.
MM	Methodist Magazine, 1798-1821, succeeded by Wesleyan Methodist Magazine from 1822.
PWHS	Proceedings of the Wesley Historical Society.

91

Chapter 1

1 JWJ, 11 May 1759.
2 JWJ, 10 April 1765; 8 April 1770, and possibly on other occasions.
3 JWJ, 7 June 1752.
4 JWJ, 11 April 1751.
5 JWJ, 8 April 1753.
6 Baker (1963), pl04, quoting *Letters* VIII, pl68.
7 Batty, p6.
8 Ibid., pp6-13.
9 Ibid.
10 Ibid.
11 Ibid.
12 Benham, p63.
13 Nelson; from which source much of the information on John Nelson has been extracted.
14 PWHS, Vol.8, pp108ff; JWJ,II, pp482-6.
15 Kirke, pp74ff.
16 Kirke, p75.
17 JBD, 30 April 1742.
18 Bennet, pp11ff.
19 Hutton, pp307ff; Benham, pp110ff.
20 Batty, pl3.
21 Baker (1963), gives additional biographical details.
22 Ibid., p95, quoting *Gillies, Historical Collections (1845 Ed.)*.
23 PWHS, Vol.13, pl09, quoting *Richard Viney Diary*.
24 PWHS, Vol.14, p14, quoting Ibid.
25 JCW, Vol.I, pp356ff.
26 PWHS, Vol.14, p84, quoting *Richard Viney Diary*.
27 Baker (1963), p95, quoting *Gillies*.

Chapter 2

1 Baker (1963), p95.
2 Jessop, p40; Everett (1827), p36.
3 MM, 1811, pp521-8.
4 Yates, p46.
5 Everett (1827), p17, where he also quotes *Myles*.
6 Haworth Book, 1749.
7 Jessop, p40.
8 PWHS, Vol.5, p37.
9 JWJ, 6 May 1747.

10 Baker Thesis, p170.
11 Ibid., p210.
12 Batty, places mentioned throughout his account. See also 'Petitions for the Registration of Inghamite Meeting Houses' extracted by the author in *North Lancashire District Methodist History Group Bulletin No.14, (January 1992)*, pp15-6.
13 Baker (1963), p236.
14 JCW, Vol.1, p440.
15 JWJ, 4-7 May 1747.

Chapter 3

1 Everett (1823), p40.
2 Rose, Vol.78, pp22-37; Vol.81, p68.
3 Minutes, 1744 & 1746.
4 Ibid., 1747.
5 JBD, 31 December 1747.
6 IGI, Yorkshire.
7 JBD, 6 August 1748.
8 Minutes, 1748.
9 JBD, 28 July 1748.
10 LRO, QSQ1, (1748).
11 Ibid.
12 Baker (1963), pp135ff; JWJ, 25 August 1748.
13 JWJ, 8 September 1750.
14 Lloyd, pp1ff.
15 PWHS, Vol.7, p80.
16 Haworth Book.
17 Baker (1963); Laycock.
18 PWHS, Vol.26, p108.
19 JBD, 18 October 1748; 10 January 1749; 18 April 1749; 11 July 1749.

Chapter 4

1 Fishwick, p337.
2 Everett (1827), pp48ff.
3 Abram, p364.
4 JBD, 3-4 January 1748.
5 JBD, 24-5 January 1748.
6 JBD, 13-5 August 1748.
7 Baker Thesis, p154, quoting *Darney*, Preface to Hymn clxii.

8 JBD, 18 September 1748; 6 October 1748; 15 April 1749.
9 LRO, QSP 1644/21.
10 Church, pp46ff; Davies, p107.
11 Dated 29 September at Newcastle.
12 JBD, 26 January 1750.
13 JBD, 23-5 January 1750.
14 Haworth Book, 1754.
15 JWJ, 8-9 June 1752.
16 JWJ, 24 April 1755.
17 MM, 1811, p524; Jessop, p54.
18 JCW, Vol.II, p128.
19 Baker Thesis, p261; Todmorden Parish Register, Burial 12 April 1759.
20 JWJ, 25 April 1755.
21 LRO, QSP 1548/24.
22 PWHS, Vol.24, pp9ff.
23 Haworth Book, 1758-61.
24 Ibid., October 1763.

Chapter 5

1 Haworth List, 1764.
2 LRO, QSP 1824/20.
3 LRO, QSP 1824/21.
4 Parish Register, Baptism 13 October 1733.
5 Taylor, pp98ff: Allen pp17ff.
6 Haworth Book, 1758-62.
7 Parish Register, Marriage 3 November 1766.
8 Richardson, p21.
9 LRO, QSP 1956/16.
10 Haworth List, 1770.
11 Anon (Bolton), p15.
12 LRO, QSP 2032/26; QDV4, 27 April 1774.
13 Taylor, pp20-7.
14 Anon (Preston), pp1ff.
15 Taylor, pp38-46.
16 Parish Register, Marriage 24 July 1781.
17 Taylor, pp28-37.
18 LRO, QSP 2164/6; 2192/15; 2196/4.
19 JWJ, 24 May 1781.
20 Taylor, p25.
21 Ibid., p44.
22 Parish Register, Marriage 29 August 1787.

23 LRO, MCo 2/2/1.
24 JWJ, 11 June 1777; Telford, Vol. VII, pp59-60.
25 LRO, MCo 2/2/1.
26 Telford, Vol.II, pp108-09.
27 PWHS, Vol.30, pp127-31.
28 Jessop, p126, quoting MM, 1845, pl6.
29 Parish Register, Marriage 10 February 1787.
30 Jessop, p127, quoting Wesley Works, Vol.XII, p488.
31 Moore, pp72-3.

Chapter 6

1 Blackburn List, 1788.
2 MM, 1812, p596.
3 Haworth List, 1764.
4 Anon (Bolton), p15.
5 LRO, QSP 1812/18.
6 Shelton, pp89-90.
7 JWJ, 27 April 1780.
8 JWJ, 18 April 1784.
9 Shelton, pp34-5.
10 JWJ, 17 April 1786.
11 Blackburn Book, 1788.
12 Ibid., 1788-94.
13 Rack, p439, quoting Field C. *The Social Structure of English Methodism in the Eighteenth to Twentieth Centuries - British Journal of Sociology XXVIII (1977).*
14 Haworth List, 1764: Blackburn List, 1790.
15 Morgan, p10; Timmins. p11.
16 Rack p441.
17 Abram, p526; Blackburn List, 1789-92; Townsend, pp29ff.
18 MM, 1839, p532.
19 Richardson, pp17ff.
20 Church (Maemp), p163.
21 Thompson, p8.
22 Blackburn List, 1791-2.
23 LRO, QSP 2316/2; DDPr 40/14.
24 LRO, QDV4, 17 January 1788.
25 Blackburn Book, 1790.
26 Nightingale, Vol.1, pp154-5, quoting Benjamin Ingham's letter of 13 March 1762.
27 Blackburn List, 1788.
28 LRO, QSP 2316/3.
29 Jackson G., p43.

30 Photocopy in my hands.
31 Blackburn Book, 1792-3.
32 LRO, QSP 2316/6.
33 Kirkman, pp63-66.
34 LRO, QSP 2296/4,
35 LRO, QDV4, 1792.
36 LRO, QSP 2332/6; 2316/5.
37 Davies, pp111-2; Walsh, pp277-89.

Chapter 7

1 Blackburn Book, 1794.
2 LRO; MF 1/72; MPr 11/1.
3 Swindlehurst, p25.
4 Blackburn List, 1790. - Richardson (p17), Taylor (p45) and others mistakenly assume that the Emmets were still living in Preston.
5 LCWHS, Vol.2, p20, (Aug.1965).
6 LCWHS, Vol.3, pp39-40, (Jan.1966).
7 Richardson, p6.
8 IGI, Northumberland.
9 LCWHS, Vol.2, p41.
10 LRO, QSP 2348/12; 2348/6-7; 2412/9. Cf Rose, Vol. 81, p88 for Preston and south of the Ribble in 1801.
11 Richardson, p21.
12 LRO, QSP 2489/9; QDV4, f44.
13 LRO, DDPr, 138/17.
14 LRO, QSP 2633/5.
15 LRO, QSP 2465/14; 2481/13; 2537/10; 2545/10.
16 Photocopy in my hands, (See page 65).
17 For additional details of the beginnings of Lancaster Methodism see LRO, MLa 1/7/3.
18 LRO, QSP 2540/76.
19 LRO, MF 1/73 for copy register of Lancaster Wesleyan.
20 LRO, QSP 2536/31
21 IGI Lancashire; Taylor, pp47-56.
22 Taylor, pp47-56 for extracts from Holden's Journal.

Chapter 8

1 LRO, QSP 2332/6.
2 Details of the Gaskell family and the other local families referred to in this chapter

have been extracted from various sources including Printed Parish Registers, Bishop's Transcripts, Probate Records, Land Tax Returns, Monumental Inscriptions, Directories, etc.

3 LRO, DDSh 4/8.
4 LRO, QSP 2348/6-7.
5 Thornber, p293.
6 LRO, QSP 2416/12.
7 LRO, QSP 2617/66.
8 LRO, MPr 11/1.
9 LRO, MF 1/71 for copy register of Garstang Wesleyan.
10 LRO, QSP 2573/13.
11 Taylor, pp51-5.
12 Extracted from Deeds held in the Circuit safe at Cleveleys.
13 Taylor, pp86-95.
14 LRO, MG (uncatalogued).
15 LRO, MBp 17/1.
16 At both the 1841 and 1851 Census approximately 54.5% of the population were in this category. The figure of 559 has been calculated by applying the same percentage to the 1831 population.
17 LRO, MGa (uncatalogued).
18 BGN, 17 March 1882.
19 MM. 1835, p62.
20 LRO, MBp 17/1.
21 LRO, MGa (uncatalogued).
22 Taylor, p35; Obituary details obtained from the Methodist Archives and Research Centre at John Rylands University Library of Manchester.

Chapter 9

1 Thornber, p209.
2 Hutton (1944), p19.
3 FC, Special Supplement, 8 November 1861.
4 Blackpool Wesleyan Methodist Circuit Handbook, October 1906.
5 Blackpool Central Library, Microfilm of 1841 Census; Rate Book for May 1841.
6 LRO, MGa (uncatalogued).
7 Blackpool South Circuit Safe, List of Trustees for 1835.
8 Ibid. Title Deeds.
9 LRO, MBp 21/3/1.
10 Blackpool South Circuit Safe, Title Deeds.
11 LRO, MGa (uncatalogued); QDV4, 1818.
12 LRO, MGa (uncatalogued).

13 Blackpool Central Library, Microfilm of 1841 Census.
14 Marton Methodist Church, Centenary Souvenir Brochure, (1972).
15 Blackpool Central Library, Microfilm of 1841 Census.
16 Taylor, p95.
17 Swift, (no pagination).
18 Blackpool Gazette and News, 11 January 1884, p3.
19 LRO, MBp 21/3/1.
20 LRO, WRW/Am, Will of Robert Baird, Proved 1851.
21 LRO, MBp 21/3/1.
22 LRO, MF 1/71 for Copy Register of Garstang Wesleyan.
23 LRO, MBp 21/3/1.
24 Ibid.
25 Ibid.
26 Ibid.
27 Ibid.
28 Ibid., FC, Special Supplement, 8 November 1861.
29 FC, Ibid. LRO, MBp 21/3/1; FC, 4 July 1962.

BIBLIOGRAPHY

Abram W.A.	*History of Blackburn,* (1877).
Allen R	*History of Methodism in Preston*, (Toulmin, Preston, 1866).
Anon (Bolton)	*Record of Early Methodism in Bolton*, by a Lay Member of the Committee, (1863).
Anon (Preston)	*Memories of an old Preston family - The Family of Crane,* (Toulmin, Preston, 1877).
Baker F	*William Grimshaw 1708-63*, Thesis for PhD, (Nottingham University).
Baker F	*William Grimshaw 1708-63*, (Epworth Press 1963).
Batty W	*An Account of Benjamin Ingham and His Work*, based on Benjamin Ingham's Diary, (John Rylands University Library, Manchester; MS Eng. 1062).
Benham D	*Memoirs of James Hutton*, (London 1856).
Bennet W	*Memoirs of Mrs. Grace Bennet*, (Macclesfield 1803).
Church L F	*The Early Methodist People*, (Epworth Press 1949).
Church L F	*More About the Early Methodist People*, (Epworth Press 1949).
Darney W	*Collection of Hymns*, (James Lister, Leeds 1751).
Davies R E	*Methodism* (Epworth Press, Rev. Ed. 1976).
Everett J	*Historical Sketches of Wesleyanism in Sheffield and its vicinity,* (Sheffield 1823).
Everett J	*Wesleyan Methodism in Manchester,* (Manchester 1827).
Fishwick H	*History of Rochdale*, (Clegg, Elliot and Stott, 1889).

Harrison A W	'Wesley's Visit to Ockbrook', *Proceedings of the Wesley Historical Society, Vol.8.*
Hutton J E	*History of the Moravian Church,* 2nd ed., (London 1809).
Hutton W	*A Description of Blackpool in 1788,* (Hodder and Stoughton, 1944).
Jackson G	*Tales of Woodplumpton and Kirkham,* (Mather Bros., c1971).
Jessop W	*Account of Methodism in Rossendale,* (Manchester 1880).
Kirke H (Ed.).	*Extracts from the Diary and Autobiography of Rev. James Clegg,* (1899).
Kirkman W	*Memorials of Mr. Thomas Crouch Hincksman,* (London c1885).
Laycock J W	*Methodist Heroes in the Great Haworth Round 1734-1784,* (Keighley 1909).
Lloyd A K	*The Labourers Hire,* (Wesley Historical Society 1968).
Moore B	*History of Wesleyan Methodism in Burnley and East Lancashire,* (Burnley 1899).
Morgan N	*Vanished Dwellings,* (Preston 1990).
Myles W	*Life and Writings of William Grimshaw,* (London 1806).
Nelson J	*Journal of John Nelson,* (1870).
Nightingale B	*Lancashire Nonconformity,* 2 Vols. (Manchester 1892).
Pilkington W	*Makers of Preston Methodism,* (1890).
Rack H D	*Reasonable Enthusiast,* (Epworth Press 1989).
Richardson W F	*Preston Methodism's 200 Fascinating Years,* (Preston 1975).
Rose E A	'Methodism in Cheshire to 1800', *Transactions of the Lancashire and Cheshire Antiquarian Society,* Vol.78, (1975).
Rose E A	'Methodism in South Lancashire to 1800', *Transactions of the Lancashire and Cheshire Antiquarian Society,* Vol.81, (1982).
Shelton E S	*Centenary Volume of the Wesleyan Methodist Chapel, Clayton Street, Blackburn,* (1886).
Swift R & Baxendale E	*Blackpool's First Free School,* (Blackpool 1991).
Swindlehurst M	*John Wesley and Wigan,* (Owl Books, Wigan 1991).
Taylor J	*The Apostles of Fylde Methodism,* (London 1885).
Telford J (Ed.)	*Wesley's Veterans,* 7 Vols. (c1910-1914).
Thompson E	*This Remarkable Family - The Barritts of Foulridge, 1750-1850,* (Barnoldswick 1981).
Thornber W	*The History of Blackpool and its Neighbourhood,* (Blackpool 1837).
Timmins J G	*Handloom Weavers Cottages in Central Lancashire,* (University of Lancaster 1977).
Townsend J	*History of Darwen Methodism,* (1916).
Yates W	*A Map of the County of Lancashire, 1786,* (Reprint Historical Society of Lancashire and Cheshire 1968).

Index of Personal Names

100

Dickinson Richard	59
Disley Lawrence	56, 78
Dobson John	80
Dobson Mary	80
Drake John	63
Drummond T	84
Dyson James	27
Earnshaw Abraham	16
Earnshaw Elizabeth	16
Edgar James	78
Edge John	30, 33
Edmondson James	6
Elston William, Rev.	66-7
Emmet Catherine	61
Emmet family	61
Emmet Michael	43-4, 46, 56, 61, 63
Emmet Michael Sr.	43
Emmet Richard	61
Emmet Thomas	63
Evans David	47
Everett (J)	16, 19, 29
Fairclough Mary	58
Fare Jane	75
Fare John	74
Fare Ellen	75
Farrer John, Rev.	89
Fazackerly William	30, 33
Field Clive, Dr.	52
Fisher Robert	57
Fishwick George	84
Fishwick Roger	38, 41
Furness John	60
Gartside Benjamin, Rev.	84-6
Gaskell Ellen	68, 71
Gaskell family	68, 72
Gaskell Isabelle	68
Gaskell John	68, 70, 75
Gaskell Joseph	68, 70
Gaskell Margaret	68
Gaskell Thomas	68, 70, 77-8
Gawkroger Joseph	12
Greenwood Betty	72, 75
Greenwood James	27
Greenwood Nanny	72, 78
Greenwood Paul	14
Greenwood Thomas	72
Greenwood William	54, 72
Grime John	37
Grimshaw Ann	13

Hunt Benjamin	61
Hunter James	35
Huntingdon Earl of	9
Huntingdon Lady	9
Hutton James	8
Hutton Thomas	60
Hutton William	80
Hyde Peggy	58
Ingham Benjamin, Rev.	7-13, 17, 19, 23, 57
Ingham William	7
Jackson Edward	48
Jackson 'Quaker'	46
Jackson Thomas	66
Jane John	22-4, 30
Jessop (William)	16
Kilham Alexander	59, 61
Knagg Richard	73
Leece Edward	88
Leece John	57, 59
Leo Miles	63
Lewtas Catherine	76-7
Lewtas George	76-7
Lewtas Jane	77
Lewtas Mary	76
Linley Mary	74
Linley Samuel	74
Livesey Joseph	66
Livesey William	38
Lyons James	58
Madin John	15-6, 27, 35
Malley Betty	75
Malley William	75
Marcer James	58-9
Marshall Major	24, 27, 35-6
Maskew Jonathan	14
Mason William	83
Mather Alexander	47
Mewburn William	86
Milner John, Rev.	6
Mitchell Thomas	41
Moon Thomas	13
Morrow James	67
Morton Thomas	38, 41
Moseley Abraham	64
Murray Grace	27
Myles (W)	16
Myers Mr.	63

❖

Index of Places

110

111

❖